The Living Spi___ ___one

TITLES IN THE SERIES

Nature, Reality, and the Sacred
Langdon Gilkey

The Human Factor
Philip Hefner

On the Moral Nature of the Universe
Nancey Murphy and George F. R. Ellis

Theology for a Scientific Age
Arthur Peacocke

The Faith of a Physicist
John Polkinghorne

The Travail of Nature
H. Paul Santmire

God, Creation,
and Contemporary Physics
Mark William Worthing

Unprecedented Choices
Audrey R. Chapman

Whatever Happened to the Soul?
Warren S. Brown, Nancey Murphy,
and H. Newton Malony, editors

The Mystical Mind: Probing the Biology
of Religious Experience
Eugene d'Aquili and
Andrew B. Newberg

Nature Reborn
H. Paul Santmire

Wrestling with the Divine
Christopher C. Knight

Doing without Adam and Eve
Patricia A. Williams

Nature, Human Nature, and God
Ian G. Barbour

In Our Image
Noreen L. Herzfeld

Minding God
Gregory R. Peterson

Light from the East
Alexei V. Nesteruk

Participating in God
Samuel M. Powell

Adam, Eve, and the Genome
Susan Brooks Thistlethwaite, editor

Bridging Science and Religion
Ted Peters and Gaymon Bennett, editors

Minding the Soul
James B. Ashbrook

The Music of Creation
Arthur Peacocke and Ann Pederson

Creation and Double Chaos
Sjoerd L. Bonting

The Living Spirit of the Crone
Sally Palmer Thomason

The Living Spirit of the Crone

Turning Aging Inside Out

Sally Palmer Thomason

FORTRESS PRESS
MINNEAPOLIS

THE LIVING SPIRIT OF THE CRONE
Turning Aging Inside Out

Cover photo: © Nanette Nanette Hooslag/Getty Images.

Library of Congress Cataloging-in-Publication Data

Thomason, Sally Palmer, 1934-
  The living spirit of the crone : turning aging inside out / by Sally Palmer Thomason.
      p. cm. — (Theology and the sciences)
  Includes bibliographical references and index.
  ISBN-13: 978-0-8006-3799-6 (alk. paper)
  ISBN-10: 0-8006-3799-2 (alk. paper)
  1. Older women—Religious life. 2. Aging—Religious aspects. I. Title. II. Series.
  BL625.7.T48 2006
  305.26—dc22
                        2006009192

The paper used in this publication meets the minimum requirements of American National Standard for Information Sciences—Permanence of Paper for Printed Library Materials, ANSI Z329.48-1984.

Manufactured in the U.S.A.

10   09   08   07   06   1   2   3   4   5   6   7   8   9   10

Contents

Preface

Crone—an old woman. Shortened from Picard *carone,* carrion, [dead and putrefying flesh] an old worn-out horse . . . a contemptuous term for a woman. . . in the sense of an old ewe.
—Skeats' Etymological Dictionary of the English Language

The Crone—the ancient holy one. She holds the powers of age and time, of retribution, and of transformation. . . . Ancient, though not always aged, she may be beautiful, but she's not pretty.
—*Ellen Lorenzi-Prince*

Within the body of the crone lies an astounding spark that Western culture through nearly three millennia has done its best to extinguish. From early childhood, our culture, through antiaging messages, scripts women to abhor the natural changes that occur in their physical appearance as they grow older. Extraordinary effort, countless hours, and untold dollars are spent by women trying to preserve their youth and to avoid looking old. It is clear that our culture influences the thoughts and behavior of aging women. A woman's attitude toward aging is largely determined by her perception of herself. How does the continual barrage of antiaging messages affect a woman's self-perception and the quality of her old age? How does our culture's view of aging as a kind of pathology shape an older woman's attitude about herself? How can she creatively and responsibly respond to this situation? This book ventures an answer to these life questions.

In my mid-sixties I embarked upon a personal quest to find the answer to these questions. Through open-ended, conversational interviews, I asked older women, ages sixty-five to ninety-two, to talk about their bodies. I was surprised that when asked about their bodies, the women I questioned did not focus primarily on the physical aspects of aging. Their responses demonstrated a more holistic view of what it means to grow old. They did talk about the physical aspects, but their answers centered more on their spiritual lives and personal relationships. Their stories bring new understanding of what gives meaning to the lives of older women. Their stories are rich and varied and demonstrate that aging, though shaped by the culture in which one lives, remains a very personal matter. Contrary to what I expected, their stories led me to a fuller appreciation of the deeply rooted connections between body, spirit, and mind in adapting to old age. Synopses of some of their stories are included in the following chapters. The names of the women have been changed to create anonymity. Also included in the book are narrative portraits created to convey the essence of what each woman talked about in her interview. Although I exercised poetic license in arrangement and emphasis, the words and phrases in these portraits are almost exclusively the narrators'.

How strange, it is, that as the population of the developed world ages, the rhetoric of medicine and merchandising has become increasingly antiaging. Stay young. Preserve youth. Find the scientific miracle to keep yourself young forever. I suspect that as a people we are losing, or have already lost, contact with the natural cycles and gifts of all life's seasons. Women moving into their middle years fear what is happening to them as their near-vision blurs, their skin wrinkles, their joints stiffen, and a visit to the doctor might bring ominous tidings. They frantically search for a bio/cosmetic fountain of youth, a miracle cure for what they perceive as the "disease" of old age, and fail to realize the potential for deeper, fuller living—yes, even joy—to be found in the spirit and body of the crone, an insight valuable not only for young and old women, but for professionals working with the elderly.

Science and theology are at a critical juncture in the understanding of human aging. Mainstream culture and bio/medical research position aging as a disease to be conquered through reductive scientific techniques, ignoring the living spirit of the individual and the essential role the numinous plays in the life of the elderly. Although within the last decade holistic, alternative, and complementary medicine and the rediscovery of ancient wisdom traditions are bringing fresh understanding to the deep interconnectedness of spirit, body, and mind, such insights are not readily accepted by established allopathic medicine. Traditional medical research, education, and practice equate old age with pathology and shape our culture's understanding of aging.

Theology has a dialectical role to play here. It can offer critical perspectives on the distortions within our popular and scientific cultures. It can recollect the vast trove of life experiences in Jewish, Christian, and other traditions and practices. It can reawaken the larger life search that can, ever more clearly, orient us to meaning and purpose as we age.

This book is thus written in the hope of shedding new light on what it means to be a crone in today's world. I could not have written it before I myself entered a new (for me) season of life and experienced the personal trials and challenges of growing old in a society that fears old age.

Chapter 1, "The Starting Point," presents personal reflections on growing old in an antiaging culture, and draws on my own increasing awareness of the inseparable nature of body, mind, and spirit. Chapter 2, "The Cultural Context," is a general survey of the demographic realities of the world's aging population, with a look at psychological development theories that shape much of our culture's current understanding of aging.

To give current attitudes toward old women a historical context, chapter 3, "Beyond Patriarchy," compares the treatment of old women within Western patriarchy to other cultural traditions. Chapter 4, "The Scientific Paradigm," reviews the tremendous variation in beliefs about old age within different cultures in different eras and traces how, within the last century, reductive, allopathic medicine led to the medicalization of aging. This positioned old age as a pathology to be treated by experts and marginalized the old as helpless and dependent. The general cultural context depicted in these two chapters is not encouraging.

However, chapter 5, "The Threshold," reveals a shifting paradigm within the medical community. New biomedical discoveries and treatments combined with holistic traditions are confirming the inseparable nature of body, spirit, and mind, and provide a different perspective on aging. Chapter 6, "Insights for Aging," explores the tremendous contribution that Carl Jung and his followers have made in helping individuals realize that stepping into old age requires a new understanding of self. During the first half of life, successful personal adjustment in our culture requires a focus outward in order to build one's ego and accommodate to the world and others. However, as one steps into old age, a reorientation inward is necessary to realize what Jung calls the *true self.* Creative old age calls for a reawakened appreciation of the mysteries and spiritual connectedness of all life.

Chapter 7, "Aging from the Inside Out," reaffirms that in today's world we may choose how we view our aging bodies and old age. We must become aware of and reject those antiaging assumptions that defy the living spirit of the crone. We must learn to appreciate our aging body in a new way—from the inside out. My personal journey led me to the ancient philosophy and practice of yoga to help me begin to comprehend the deep interconnections of body, mind, and spirit within all of life.

Although it is impossible to acknowledge and thank all those who have helped in the writing of this book, I have special thanks for a few. Long before I ever knew the meaning of the word *crone*, my father inspired me to believe in myself and cultivated knowledge that there were great truths to be found beneath and beyond the superficial. My mother's practical guidance led me to respect and care for my body and appreciate the world around me. My daughters and granddaughters enlivened my realization of what it means to be woman in today's world. When I started my research into aging at the age of sixty-five, I was guided and stretched by my doctoral committee, and I am most grateful for the advice and support of Thomas McGowan, Jill Jones, Rita Arditti, Sherry Penn, Judith Arcana, Lea Gaydos, and Donn Bree.

At the center of everything I have written are the stories of the women whom I interviewed. They remain anonymous because of our agreement. However, their willingness to share their experiences, feelings, and thoughts was my inspiration. Phyllis Tickle's professional advice and guidance furnished the prod needed to keep me writing. The encouragement of my friends Mary Reed, Lila Saunders, Suzy Mallory, Shelley Griffee, Stephanie Harrover, Ann Kerr and Linda Douty, who read and commented on my manuscript, was invaluable. Were it not for the editor of this series, Kevin Sharpe, and the extraordinary woman who is his wife and my mentor (though half my age), Leslie Van Gelder, this book never would have seen print. And, most of all, I thank my first reader, best friend, confidant, love, and husband, John Thomason, who when I started this project was not sure where I was going but always gave wholehearted support to my endeavor.

1

The Starting Point

The only true voyage of discovery is not to go to new places but to have other eyes.
—*Marcel Proust*, Remembrance of Things Past

The universe exists as seen through the eyes of the individual.
—*Ralph de Vito*

The train pulled slowly to a hissing stop as I pushed open the heavy glass and steel door to jump down onto the concrete platform. Where was I? It was a foreign depot, one I did not know. I made my way through the bustling crowd and entered the cavernous, domed-ceiling station of an unknown city. Faceless travelers rushed in all directions, keenly intent on their destination and oblivious to me. Standing alone, knowing no one, and not sure where I was, I realized I had arrived without luggage. Frantically, I turned to work my way back through a labyrinth of dark, winding narrow tunnels to where I thought I had left my bags. They were not there.

I was having a lot of extraordinary dreams the week before my sixty-fifth birthday. The next night I dreamed I was in the midst of a large, fancy-dress celebration in a radiantly festooned hall where friends were helping me assemble my most prized belongings in an elegant bag. Something distracted me for an instant. When I turned again to the task, my friends and the suitcase we were loading with my accumulated treasures had disappeared.

Dream experts say that every part of our dreams represents a part of our psyche—our unconscious selves expressed in metaphor. Some say a dream is a message from God. So what was going on in my unconscious? What was my message? Was I lost or abandoned, or was it time to get rid of worn-out baggage, my trove of accumulated trappings, and find new, lightweight, travel-friendly effects for the next stage of my journey?

Probably a little of both.

Stepping into Old Age

An individual's age, reckoned in quantitative terms as the number of years one has lived, is perhaps the most noted and relied-upon marker in our society. Everyone must know his or her age. Although we tend to identify our name as our label, our age is far more reliable for fitting us into the larger picture. It is a universal distinguishing feature of identification, the ever-present question on the many and varied forms and questionnaires we fill out—from school enrollment, a doctor appointment, a credit application, to marketing surveys. Age determines our eligibility for Social Security and the price we pay at the movies; it even determines the movies we can see. Our legal eligibility to drive a car, vote, have an alcoholic drink, join the army, or fill out a marriage license without parental approval—all are based on our age. Statisticians, insurance actuaries, biomedical researchers, market analysts, government planners, politicians, sociologists, criminologists, psychologists, and educators spew out table after table of demographic information to chart the expected state and behavior of a single human being at a particular age in his or her life journey.

Yet the older I get, the less I believe in those numbers. I have found that aging is an extremely individual enterprise. Waneen Spirduso, a physiologist at the University of Texas, agrees. In her definitive study of the physical dimensions of aging, she found that the longer a person lives, the greater that person's observable diversity. Dr. Spirduso concluded that the "typical" old person does not exist—the manner and quality of aging clearly depend on the individual. There is a vast difference in the attributes and behaviors of people and *the way they change over time*. (Although debilitating conditions are often present with aging, the causes for these debilities are not clearly understood, and not all old people have them. Well-documented research on hundreds of subjects shows that chronological age is *not* a good predictor of function or performance.) Aging is a highly individualized process.[1]

Learning Aging

I celebrated my sixtieth birthday a year before I retired from full-time employment as dean of continuing education at a small liberal arts college in a large metropolitan area. I enjoyed my work, but a growing desire to be free from administrative hassles and a gnawing spirit to explore new horizons made me know it was time for a change.

Yet when I retired, although I felt full of life and health, I sensed a nuance of difference in the way friends and former colleagues treated me. I wondered what they meant when they said I deserved a good rest. True, I wanted a change, but I wasn't ready to be put out to pasture, or to withdraw from active participation in life. Even though I had given up running a couple of years earlier because of so much pain in my knee, I still played tennis a couple of times a week and was in good health. It occurred to me that perhaps I was projecting my own uneasiness onto what they were saying. After all, I had personally reached the age in which our society begins to label a woman "old." I had to admit that at many levels this was scary. Strictly speaking, I was already a crone, an older woman no longer capable of bearing children, having experienced menopause five or six years earlier. (Strangely, I cannot pinpoint the exact dates of that life-defining change about which so much is written. I went through that significant passage with little physiological or psychological upset, even though for years I had been warned that it would be a terrible, upsetting milestone.)

As I moved into my sixth decade and was no longer employed full-time, however, I found myself confronting what it means to be an old woman in a society that fears old age and glorifies youth. I was beginning to experience what it meant to be a crone in a culture that expends millions of dollars annually on face-lifts, hair color, and Botox. Although Webster defines *old* simply as having lived many years (no negative connotation there), the very word *old* has pejorative implications—something akin to worn out, no longer of use. American culture equates *old* with negativity and loss. Young women barely into their twenties complain about getting old, as if elusive youth is only granted to those in adolescence. Why, in our culture, is life for a woman beyond pubescence so tinged with fear and dread?

My sixtieth birthday pulled me into a quantitative analysis of my life. Looking at today's provocative statistics, in the United States and other technically advanced societies, a healthy woman in her seventh decade can reasonably anticipate an additional thirty to forty years, since the number of centenarians are increasing annually. As I thought back over the amazing amount of living I had experienced in the two previous thirty-year periods of my life, I marveled at how different in associations and activities one was from the other. To live creatively for the next thirty years would be a challenge requiring new learning, new perspectives, new understandings, and new skills. Had I been born in 1834 instead of 1934, my chances of reaching even my fortieth birthday would have been slim. Today, in terms of years, I still face the equivalent of living an entire nineteenth-century lifetime, having already experienced infancy, childhood, and a good portion of adulthood. The twenty-first century offers three lives in the span of what once was one.

Although I was not facing early childhood developmental tasks or midlife adjustments, I realized I had a parallel challenge. If I was going to get the most out of my upcoming "lifetime," I needed to appreciate the changes in my situation, my self, and my relationships. Maybe those dreams were telling me something. I needed to pack new bags—learn new ways, meet new challenges, gain new knowledge, hone new skills, adapt to new realities, and decide what outworn baggage I should leave behind.

Such new learning is not instinctive. Our culture did not prepare me, or any of my contemporaries, to make this type of reassessment to find new attitudes and behavior at this stage of life. Cultural assumptions and traditions say that when we reach sixty-five we are supposed to step out of the mainstream, exercise our senior-citizen rights and benefits, settle into AARP-discounted buffets, retell the stories of the glory days of our youths, and share the "lessons of life" with grandchildren more interested in video games than in us. In a society where one's worth is judged by what she or he produces, we are given a heartfelt send-off, presented a gold watch or its equivalent, and gently shoved to the sidelines, where we are tacitly categorized as social drones and an economic drain. When I left the time pressures and stress of a regular job commitment, I began to wonder how much of this negative attitude toward aging was subliminally buried in my own psyche. I realized it was very important for me to know how I myself felt about growing old.

Becoming Aware of Our Assumptions

"I don't feel *old*. In fact, I feel younger now than I did years ago."

I was at a natural spirituality dream-group session at our church. The associate minister spoke those words to eight women she was leading in exploring new ways to connect with their spiritual essence. Establishing the group took courage and raised some conservative eyebrows. She was well grounded in her approach, however. Over the years she had survived repeated harsh blows of personal tragedy—a husband killed in an auto crash, leaving her with three infant children; in more recent times, a son's death from AIDS. Yet an indomitable spirit and growing faith transformed her from a tragic victim filled with grief and loss to an exemplar of spiritual leadership, exuding inspiration and hope.

Her words resounded in my head. What was she saying? What was the meaning of that statement coming from a woman who, through example, gave strength and vitality to our group of aging women? *I don't feel old*, implying, "I don't feel bad, worn out, decrepit, degenerate." *I feel young*, implying, "I feel full of life, energetic, active, attractive."

Enculturated habits of word usage convey meanings of which we are not aware. When we listen carefully to the words we use, the stories we tell, and the declarations we make, we learn a great deal about our basic beliefs. We uncover the value system the culture in which we live tacitly and subliminally imprints upon us. It never occurs to us to question the meaning of our words. It is part of our reality. My friend's words conveyed the very culturally inscribed meanings from which she had escaped. In her early sixties she felt full of life, energetic, active, and attractive. Why did she choose the word *young*, which essentially means not far advanced in years—immature—to express positive attributes about herself? What did she mean when she declared that she did not feel *old*?

What we unconsciously accept and act on as true comes from basic values and beliefs that are built and reinforced within our culture over a long period of time. Charles Tart, a contemporary psychologist, coined the phrase *consensus trance* to describe the half-conscious state in which everyone within a given culture unquestioningly and unknowingly accepts the values, belief system, and view of reality of that culture.[2] Since a culture's belief system is deeply embedded, historically reinforced, and tacitly assumed to be true, my friend was not aware of her own consensus trance that old is bad and young is good.

Opening our minds in an effort to discern and identify culturally constructed values is challenging and difficult. Habits of thought and speech are deeply entrenched. For example, as one grows older, memory lapses are often attributed to aging. When I cannot remember the name of an acquaintance, I am tempted to ascribe my lapse, as do many of my contemporaries, to a "senior moment." In fact, however, I never was good at remembering names. Short-term memory does not necessarily deteriorate with age. That it must do so is a well-entrenched myth. (Indeed, recent research ascribes the slowing down of recall to the fact that human brains in time become loaded with so much information that it takes longer to sort through the data.) A study by Harvard psychologist Ellen Langer and her colleague Rebecca Levy confirms that the belief in the loss of memory is a cultural myth based on stereotyping old age.

> The researchers studied two populations of people who hold their elders in high esteem—elderly mainland Chinese and older, deaf Americans—and compared them to a group of elderly mainstream Americans. In addition, the researchers compared memory retention in the elderly with younger people in all three groups. Not only did the mainland Chinese and American deaf far outperform the mainstream Americans on four psychological memory tests, but the oldest in these two groups, especially the Chinese, performed almost as well as the youngest. Their performance was so strong even the researchers were surprised. They conclude that the results can be explained entirely by the fact that the Chinese have the most positive, active, and "internal" image of aging across the three cultures studied.[3]

The current collective view of aging is so relentlessly negative, however, that the fear of memory loss becomes a self-fulfilling prophecy. Vigilant awareness—the deliberate, nonjudgmental observation of what we say and think, is the first essential to cultivate, to pack in our portmanteau for this new phase in our journey. We need conscientiously to observe what we say, do, and think if we want to recognize our cultural programming. When we become alert to preconceptions that color our thinking, we begin to appreciate how our minds process our perceptions of events and people; we begin to notice the unsolicited feelings and thoughts that arise from the repository of experience and beliefs that reside within us. When we are not alert, these preconceptions lead to automatic evaluations or action and shape our attitudes about aging and ourselves.

Sociologist William Sadler says our culture identifies aging with the *D* words: *decline, disease, dependency, depression*, and *decrepitude*.[4] To his list I add denial. We are living longer, but what good are more years of living if we expect sickness and suffering and want to hide our age? Although the *D* words define the view of aging most often portrayed in the popular media, the living reality of many older people does not support these assumptions. To dispel myths and see new realities about old age requires that we throw out many of the entrenched expectations and ideas that for years we have accepted without question. We must learn to recognize destructive *habits* of thought.

Susan Heidrich, from the School of Nursing at the University of Wisconsin, conducted important longitudinal studies on self-perceptions in aging women. She found that deteriorating physical conditions or diminished financial resources seemed to have little effect on these women's satisfaction with life in general. Heidrich found that physical health did not predict change over time in purpose in life, personal growth, or autonomy. Other studies confirm her findings. Aging adults, for the most part, are able successfully to neutralize the effects of disadvantages on themselves and maintain a consistent, satisfying lifestyle through a sense of personal agency and adaptation.[5] Although older folks change and adapt to physical limitations, Heidrich found yet another factor that struck a damaging blow to the sense of self in the older women she interviewed. She concluded that the changes in self-perceptions among the older women she interviewed were due to advancing age.[6] This finding demands careful consideration. If it is not physical health or reduced circumstances that change an older person's self-concept, is it the expectations and beliefs about aging itself that diminish personal growth, a sense of purpose and ability, and a desire to foster new relationships? Do the beliefs of an elder about old age become a self-fulfilling prophecy? How can we foster a new view of old age?

By the time we have lived more than sixty years, we see ourselves according to established expectations. We have "confirmed" notions about the way things are. Sadly, these expectations, even when not true, influence one's self-concept and can dramatically reduce life satisfaction in later years. Culturally entrenched expectations about old age are the useless baggage that we must discard. Learning how to open our hearts and minds to new possibilities is the challenge for our ongoing journey into old age. Refusing to apply general beliefs about aging to oneself is probably the most important decision an aging individual can make.

The Beginner's Mind

One way to create fresh awareness and understanding is to start with what the Zen masters call "a beginner's mind."

> Beginner's mind is Zen practice in action. It is the mind that is innocent of preconceptions and expectations, judgments and prejudices. Beginner's mind is just present to explore and observe and see "things as-it-is." [sic] I think of beginner's mind as the mind that faces life like a small child, full of curiosity and wonder and amazement. "I wonder what this is? I wonder what that is? I wonder what this means?" Without approaching things with a fixed point of view or a prior judgement [sic], just asking "what is it?"[7]

Cultivating a beginner's mind is difficult at any age. Because we increasingly are burdened by preconceptions the longer we live, the cultivation of a beginner's mind is even harder as we approach old age. We have tried new things many times and "know" what works and what does not. It is sometimes very arduous to muster the desire or marshal the energy to make changes in later life or even to believe that we can. It is too easy to tell ourselves that it really doesn't matter. Relying exclusively on what we have learned in the past, we unwittingly sabotage ourselves.

Recently I witnessed how an older friend's sophisticated, cultivated judgment undermined his personal resolve. In his eightieth year, mentally alert and physically agile, Dave decided to revive a long-dormant passion for playing the violin. He had shown considerable aptitude as a youth but in his late teens abandoned the violin in favor of other interests. When he retired from his third career—the first in advertising, the next in retail executive management, and the third as a college professor—he recognized the necessity for active new learning at this transitional point in his life.

He began weekly violin lessons with a regular practice schedule. Yet after six months he quit. He could not countenance the dreadful noise he was making. His ear for music, cultivated over a lifetime of listening, did not allow him to bring a beginner's mind or ear to his practice. Now possessing a full appreciation of the exquisite sound produced by a virtuoso, he felt only disappointment and dismay as he evaluated his own progress. He could not refrain from judging himself by an established standard of perfection, which brought him keen disappointment.

Perhaps his fingers lacked the necessary dexterity ever again to play the violin well, or perhaps he could not give himself the same tolerance that his mother or his neighbors must have shown when as a little boy he made his first squeaking attempts on unforgiving strings. We expect novice mediocrity and youthful failures as the immature develop a skill. It is very difficult, however, for an older person to allow him- or herself the same preliminary period of development when trying to become proficient. Also, all too often, we have lost the knack of play, of taking joy in the process, as we continually and critically evaluate the product.

Our resolve is colored by an untrue but pervasive cultural assumption that "you can't teach an old dog new tricks." Queen Victoria learned the Russian language in her eighties. A woman in my yoga class accomplished a lifetime first—an unassisted full-arm balance (on the playground when I was ten, we called it a handstand) when she was sixty-eight. She had started the practice at sixty-two and stood on her head for the first time in her life at sixty-five. New learning is possible at any age, but the false notion that no new learning takes place after a certain age discourages older people from cultivating new skills or even attempting something new.

New learning is possible at any age, but it is not easy. Proficiency takes time, discipline, commitment, and patience. Developing a skill requires months, usually years, of dedicated practice. (Twenty years ago my husband and I took a four-month sabbatical in Germany. We wanted to learn the language, so we spent the first month in an intensive language course at the Goethe Institute in Blaubauren. We both had an introductory knowledge of the language and expected to be fully conversant within four weeks. Our expectations were unrealistic. We spend a lifetime learning our native language yet never fully master it, so we fell far short of our goal but had a wonderful time.) After the first step, which is the decision to start, a beginner's mind helps one have a direct experience and avoid the discouragement of judging progress against preconceived standards. The mantra for this stage of life is the Zen master's words: "In the beginner's mind there are many possibilities, but in the expert's mind there are few." A beginner's mind encourages us to find pleasure in the process, reawakening a sense of play, illuminating our ideas and activities with a different light as we begin to see through a different lens. A beginner's mind helps us become more aware of the many possibilities that exist with a new view of old age.

Re-membering the Body, Mind, and Spirit

Of course we cannot deny that aging changes our bodies. Aging radically alters our appearance—the way we look to others, the way we look to ourselves. Many of these changes cause pain and slow us down. Yet when we do not recognize that the physical matter of our being is integral and deeply interconnected to our mind and spirit, we fail truly to access the untapped wisdom that lies deep within each individual. A wisdom that will furnish guidance, never all the answers, for one's journey into old age is what we seek.

When I began my exploration of aging, I wanted to know how older women view their bodies and to consider how their culture influences their perceptions of themselves as they age, which in turn shapes the quality of their aging. Believing that I would gain deeper insight through open-ended conversations using naturalistic, qualitative methodology for my research, I established a definite focus but no specific questions. I wanted to hear how the women themselves shape their understanding of their aging bodies. As Max Van Manen counsels, one should approach inquiry of a lived experience "not as a problem in need of a solution but a mystery in need of evocative comprehension."[8] As I talked with older women about their bodies, they did not limit their narrative to the biophysical reality of their beings, and I came to a far richer understanding of the multifaceted meanings of their lives. The women I questioned did not focus primarily on the physical aspects of aging. Their responses demonstrated a more holistic view of what it means to grow old. They talked about the physical, but their answers centered more on their spiritual life and personal relationships. Their stories gave me enlarged insights into what brings meaning to older women's lives. They clearly demonstrated there is no such thing as a "typical" old woman and underscored the reality that aging is a very personal matter. Contrary to what I expected, I found many crones not only celebrate "wearing purple," but lead the way to a new understanding of the deep-rooted connections between body, spirit, and mind.

Nora and I met one afternoon in late January at the yoga studio where we both attend a weekly session. Before this meeting we had only exchanged casual greetings at the beginning and end of class, but when I telephoned her to ask if she would participate in my study, she was interested and willing. She suggested that we meet at the yoga studio during a time when no classes were scheduled so we would be alone. Open talk of the body requires a safe place. The studio was a good, neutral, private spot where we would not be interrupted. The room was chilly when we entered. We grabbed a couple of blankets, wrapped them around our shoulders, and, absent chairs, sat Indian style on the floor.

She had thought a great deal about her body, was interested in my questions, and was eager to share with me a life-changing experience she had in her mid-fifties. At seventy-one she felt more energy and enthusiasm for living than she could remember ever having before. Her renewal started when she was in her sixties, a decade she thoroughly enjoyed. But before exploring recent times, our talk retreated from the present so she could start her story at the beginning.

Nora's Story

Nora was born and grew up in a very small town in east Tennessee with a population of less than two hundred folks. The little village, nestled in the foothills of the Smoky Mountains had no high school, so Nora traveled daily by bus just over the state line into Kentucky for her secondary education and attended the University of Tennessee at Knoxville, where she earned a Bachelor of Science in Education. Although she left her rural roots when she was eighteen, Nora remarked that where she grew up colored her whole existence. She felt a deep, abiding connection to nature and the land.

After college she taught for four years, got married, moved to Wisconsin for her husband's job, bore and reared two sons, moved to Memphis when her husband was again transferred, and for the past forty-five years had lived in the same house in a quiet suburban neighborhood. As Nora thinks back over those years, they are a blur. "I wasn't really there then. I feel like I was so unaware of what I was doing."

She talked of being a wife and mother, having children; yet not being fully conscious of herself in her activities, she felt almost as if she lived by rote. She expressed no regrets, just a vague uneasiness about what she may have missed during a great lapse of time, living life on autopilot—unconscious, not really engaging fully in her life at that time.

While in Wisconsin Nora became pregnant with her first child. She went into labor at six months, and the doctor questioned whether there could have been some mistake as to the date of conception. Once it was established the reckoning was accurate, he said, "You know, this baby can't live." So accepting the inevitable, Nora was prepped for the birth. The baby boy came out crying, weighing only two pounds, pitifully thin, but breathing. He remained in the hospital for two months, but he lived. The doctor told Nora, "Frankly, it was the nuns who saved him." The nuns rocked him every night, and nestled him in their arms, bringing the warmth of human touch and love to his nascent life. At the same time, Nora was not allowed even to lay a finger on her baby, let alone rock him. She never held her baby during those two months he was in the hospital. At the time she never questioned the doctor's orders or the hospital's policy. She says she and her child did not bond.

Forty years later obstetricians and pediatricians know the vital importance of early touch and bodily contact for the bonding of mother and child, and for the health of each. In the 1950s they did not. While the benefits of human touch for subsequent security and development of the infant are now well documented, what is not so widely understood are the emotional effects of hormonal changes on new mothers at the time of birth. There is a neuro-biological base for the "infatuation" a new mother feels for her newborn. Near the time of birth, as the body readies itself for delivery, a hormone called oxytocin, produced in the hypothalamus, is secreted into the bloodstream. The release of oxytocin stimulates nerve messages that create mild, pleasant sexual sensations through the mother's body. The very sight, sound, and smell of her newborn activate a warm, contented arousal within the mother—nature's way of promoting the vitalizing force of maternal care and bonding.[9] When this natural maternal urge is denied, there are lasting consequences for the mother. Today Nora is amazed that she compliantly acquiesced to the doctor's orders, suppressing the natural call of her body to cuddle her baby.

And ignoring the wisdom of her body was the course she followed for the next thirty years. Fortunately, she was healthy. Relatively unconcerned, she saw her body as nothing more than the mechanism to support what she wanted to do. When there was illness she called on the expertise of a medical doctor and willingly consumed his (in those days they were usually men) prescriptions and followed his advice.

At a routine check-up, when Nora was in her late fifties, the doctor heard an abnormality in her heart. There was a slight mitral-valve prolapse, but he assured her that in her case it was not a problem, only an individual idiosyncrasy much like blue or brown eyes. What Nora heard was that she had a problem with her heart. She was terrified. Her heart was her link to life, and she thought she was going to die. In spite of what the doctor said, she had her own ideas. Nora believed that if she did anything to strain her heart that would be the end. Nobody could convince her otherwise. She went to bed for nine months.

Looking back, she realizes she could not hear what the doctor was telling her. She wasn't listening. Her reaction was an emotional culmination of a ten-year buildup that started with her mother's death, followed four years later by her older sister's death, and then three years later with the death of her father. All of her closest kin were gone. Her shock was palpable. Now, Nora thought it was her turn. "I went through, what do you call it? A dark night of the soul." She had always been in good health. A minor physical anomaly triggered a major emotional breakdown.

"It felt like my body had betrayed me. I was always so healthy and felt so good, and all of a sudden my body wasn't functioning. I won't say I hated it, but I was very perplexed. I really think it was my emotional state that was causing the problem. It just happened to coincide with the physical." Nora said there were actually three things: her father's death, her physical body acting up, not doing what she wanted it to do, and her emotions that just "snowballed."

Like an injured animal, Nora retreated from her normal activities into a safe, dark hole, her bedroom. Like the Greek goddess Persephone, who went deep into the underworld to meet the demons and integrate her soul, Nora withdrew from engagement in her exterior life. She went deep within and in time confronted her inner self—her submerged needs, impulses, and desires. She remembers that at the point of her deepest despair, she came to understand that she had a choice as to how she lived her life. After nine months, the same period as human gestation, she slowly emerged, "transformed, like a new being." "It was like I kind of came out of a tunnel. I was almost into my sixties, and I felt like I really hadn't done anything worthwhile as an individual. . . . But then my life just kind of opened up."

Musing aloud about those nine months of what she now calls depression, Nora asked me if I thought this kind of crisis happened normally to everyone. Nora's question reminded me of D. Patrick Miller's words,

> They say there are no atheists in foxholes; I would add that there are not many with a long sojourn on a sickbed on their résumé. The spiritual conversion experience that often visits those who have hit rock bottom due to illness, addiction, or depression can be looked at in two ways: either people crack under the pressure and take flight from their senses, or they crack under the pressure and catch a healing glimpse of a new reality. Reviewing my own experience over the past sixteen years, I would say that both perspectives are correct. You have to go a little nuts to begin looking at the world in a whole new way, and that style of seeing can have an authentic healing effect.[10]

Nora said her sixties, the decade just past, were the most "fun years" of her life. She "discovered" her work becoming a full-time volunteer coordinator for a community garden—digging in the soil, attuning to the seasons, nurturing growth, helping others learn about gardening, and connecting with her long-lost childhood affinity with nature. She has an easy, loving relationship with all of her family, including that premature firstborn, who is now a middle-aged, "slightly overweight" father of two teenagers.

A niece took her—"practically drug me"—to a yoga class. The niece soon dropped out, but Nora became a regular. She not only stretched and strengthened her muscles, but she became aware of her body in a very different way. She began paying attention to what her body was telling her and quit taking it for granted, or just placing its care in the hands of a medical doctor. In a new and vital way, she understood that she was responsible for her health and needed conscientiously to work to maintain it. Reflecting on how unaware of her body she had been in younger years, she said, "My body was just something that took me where I wanted to go." Through the disciplined practice of yoga she learned to be aware of her body from the inside out and more and more realized the deep connection between body, mind, and soul all working together. Dropping into a more reflective tone, she talked about how she had become more comfortable living on the edge of uncertainty; since one could never know what "tomorrow" will bring, she found it essential to focus on what is happening now, today, in the moment.

Though friendly and at ease with other people, Nora is a very private person; Nora is very much a child of her time. In her generation "nice" girls did not talk about their bodies. We met in the safety of the yoga studio, and she knew that I was receptive to that practice and philosophy, so she readily shared her ideas and experience with me. But she does not readily talk about yoga. She knows the practice is making her much stronger. She really feels good and mentioned that the other day a friend asked her, "Do you feel as good as you look?" But she did not tell her friend about yoga. She was not sure what the friend would think. Nora is afraid that people, particularly those with whom she works, will think she belongs to some strange cult. She was happy that our interview was anonymous. She does not believe that those with whom she has daily contact would understand her interest in yoga or her "tranformative" experience. She fears censure, being labeled "a kook." Her new awareness is not easily shared, for she still functions socially in the culture of her past. At least she perceives that her past shapes her relations to others and does not want to upset the balance.

Even though Nora does not freely share her personal journey and may live socially in two separate worlds, she rejoices in her new, holistic understanding of mind, body, and spirit. The words she uses to describe the experience of coming forth from depression into a joyous engagement with life capture this new understanding—*the infinite self re-members itself*. Today she feels whole.

After my conversation with Nora, I sketched the following word portrait, using only Nora's words.

It took sixty years to re-member my body, my mind, my soul.
They have been with me all my life, I just never took notice.

Heck, my life course was set.
I was active.
I was attractive.
I got my education.
I got my man.
Life carried me along; things were as they were.
Okay with me. That's how it goes.

My first son was born needing radical care.
"Too small to make it," but he did.
Contained in my body the first six months, Sisters of Mercy
    supported his next two.
The doctor said no touch for me, while others cradled his
    nascent life.
We did not bond.
Okay with me. That's how it goes.

Gray is the color of my next thirty years.
I know I was there, numb but not unhappy.
Things were as they were.
Okay with me. That's how it goes.

My sister's, then my mother's, death shocked me from the
    haze into despair.
Why am I alive?
What can all this mean?
My heart became the trickster.
I too was going to die.

Terrified I lay abed nine months.
Though my body sent forth sons before their time, my soul
　　required full-term gestation.
Ears and eyes locked shut to the world about, I was
　　unconscious of the mysterious forces working in my
　　soul.
The alchemy of transformation lies beyond the rational—
　　first comes awareness.
I have a dream, a recurring dream—downtown with others I
　　start home and realize I took the wrong direction.
Jung says a dream is a messenger from the soul.

In my sixties I woke up, transformed and ready for the task of
　　re-membering my body, mind, and soul.
A newfound consciousness filled my being.
Awake and alive I found my work.
I found my life.
Connecting through the soil to all things living, a new
　　meaning unfolded within.
I love my work in the community garden.

Through yoga I learned to listen to the wisdom of my body.
I connected with the joy of disciplined awareness.
I rejoice in my newfound flexibility toward life.
I am *re-membered* and rejoice.

Nora's re-membering of her body, mind, and spirit was a transformative experience. It gave her a new perspective on her life. On the threshold of her croneship she retreated deep within herself, afraid to get out of bed, afraid of life, afraid of death. At her lowest point, she realized she had a choice to live beyond the role ordained by her culture and situation. She became aware of the cultural assumptions that had molded her into a frightened woman. It was at this lowest point that she took up the challenge to bring forth the parts of herself that had been submerged and repressed for years. Nora began her creative journey into wholeness, where she gained new understanding, started new activities, and found joy in the new stage of her life.

An Individual Matter

Trying to comprehend the multiple and mysterious facets of aging is like trying to embrace a giant amoeba. When squeezed in one area, it squirts out and dribbles off in another direction, never taking definite form, always eluding precise definition. On reflection, this is not surprising, for the process of aging mirrors both the subject and object—the living, changing, organic process of *life* itself.

As I talk with older women I honor the fact that values and beliefs and the factors that shape those beliefs are embedded in the words they use and the stories they tell. When asked a specific question, their responses reflect their lived experience. My interview with eighty-year-old Suzy was typical. I asked her how she perceived her body. She asked for clarification: "Are you talking about the physical body or the mental attitude?" I said I wanted to know what she meant when she said the word *body*. She mused aloud, and we talked for over two hours. Her individual story was alive with meaning as she told me about the "matters" of her life. I saw her spirit fill her definition of her body.

Extemporaneous stories from other women give profound testimony to the reality that personal meaning is situated in place, time, and culture. Amanda grew up in the mountains of east Tennessee and is deeply rooted in her matrilineal Cherokee heritage. She views her body and old age very differently than does Gay, raised during the Depression in a traditional, male-oriented environment in Madison, Wisconsin, or Martha, who spent her early years in China where her parents were missionaries. We all have a story within. If we listen carefully, we find clues of what we value and who we are becoming. So having collected personal stories from other women, I next set out to discover what my story would reveal about my aging body.

My Story

Today when I stand in front of the mirror and stare at my reflected image, the body I present to the world, I am struck with how little I see of who I am. My thoughts, my feelings, my memories are the me that I know—not the reflection before me. The material form I see has familiar features but with strange contradictions. I am fascinated and imagine a kaleidoscope of images that whirl back through the years presenting a freckle-faced, pigtailed ten-year-old, a self-conscious teenager frantic to hide the emerging pimple on her chin, a fresh-faced young bride absorbed with the face that attracted the love of her life, a harassed mother who locked the bathroom door to gain three minutes of privacy away from the squabbling toddlers in the next room, the time-pressed professional converting frizzy hair to waves with the heat of a curling iron, the mother of the bride in her electric-blue silk dress touching up her mascara before leaving for the church, and the wrinkled-faced crone who takes pride that she can still fit into the Harris tweed suit she bought forty years ago in Dublin (if she does not button the waistband).

How could Descartes have been so wrong? I breathe, see, sing, cry, dance, make love, have babies, play tennis, play cards, earn money, make speeches, shop, sew, hurt people, make people happy. I read, I meditate, I pray. I despair over five pounds gained on vacation, the distancing of a once robust friendship, the failure to have sufficient funds in my checking account at the end of the month, a grown child's choice to distance himself emotionally and geographically, an arthritic knee.

I listen on the phone to a daughter dealing with the disappointment that life is not perfect, that husbands argue, children rebel, choices are hard, and people are sometimes nasty. I listen to the excitement in my husband's voice as he reads the laudatory comments a friend wrote about his just-published book. I feel the release of tension in my stiff back as I stretch down to touch my toes and straddle into the yoga pose of a downward dog. I revel in the written words of an author who captures an elusive truth I have longed to articulate. I get a shiver up my spine when the neighbor's three-month-old baby grasps my finger and won't let go. I grieve over the cancer and subsequent loss of a dear friend. I thrill that after years of watching the setting sun paint the clouds with exuberant lavender pinks, muted mauves, and pale saffron I finally see "the green flash" as the golden orb slips beneath the horizon. I savor biting through the skin of a firm Fuji apple and the first sip from a cup of freshly ground French-roast coffee. I stagger with the stiffness in my joints after sitting too long in one position. I marvel at the carefully reasoned exposition of quantum theory or descriptive analysis of a recent biochemical discovery. I bow my head in gratitude for the wonders of my life.

Because of all this and much, much more, I live, Mr. Descartes; therefore, I am.

To consider body apart from self is absurd. Every part, every experience, every thought, every relationship, every sensation makes me who I am, from the moment of conception until my last breath, maybe beyond. Through seventy years—gaining a completely new set of cells every seven years—I've changed shape, size, physical and mental capacity, interests, activities, relationships, responsibilities, and place innumerable times. I have taken on a number of various identities—toddler, playmate, daughter, niece, student, cheerleader, traveler, hostess, wife, homemaker, mother, worker, boss, teacher, aunt, runner, friend, volunteer, sailor, neighbor, pilot, writer, mountain climber, grandmother. Yet through them all, the physical matter, the functioning mind and numinous spirit, with its millions of complex, interlaced manifestations from depression through ecstasy, maintained a composite oneness—the protean me.

From my earliest impressions, no longer retrievable from memory but intuited from later experience, my body and I were one. At five, a skinned knee hurt me through and through, engaging the whole me—my dignity as well as my leg was injured. On mature reflection I realize at that early age I must have honored the sanctity of my flesh. I cried but tolerated the washing of the wound and blew away the sting as my mother applied the iodine. I trusted, even though I did not understand, that far worse would happen if infection invaded through this open tear. My world was secure and, although an occasional paddling from my father bruised my bottom as well as my sense of justice, as a child my body, mind, spirit, and world were neatly intertwined; I had not yet apprehended distinction between the "me and the non-me world."[11]

Perhaps the first crack in my holistic perception came when the curly-headed boy, who prided himself as being the class wit, wrote in my first-grade autograph book, "This summer you had better reduce, if you want to catch any wolves on the loose." We were best friends, so I paid little heed. We walked the three blocks together to and from school every day, and I knew he was just being funny. But at some level his admonition must have made a deep impression. Why else would I remember the silly little verse sixty-five years later?

Sometime before my eleventh year a new kind of body awareness crept into my consciousness. Rather than undifferentiated acceptance of me—the total package—I began to compare my body to the bodies of my friends. Many of my girlfriends were sprouting bosoms, while my chest remained as flat as my brother's. Nightmares of being caught in public with no blouse, revealing to the world my deficiency, are my first memory of a different view of my body—a self-image based on another image—how I looked to someone else.

Within a couple of years, as my upper body began to display feminine curvature, I was profoundly relieved. Yet concern over and attention to my weight, my clothes, the shade of my lipstick, and the length of my hair occupied much of my life. The opinions of others were molding the way I viewed my body, and it took years for me even to recognize what was happening. I was lucky. These concerns were not my whole. I played, studied sometimes, learned, enjoyed girlfriends, felt romantic attraction toward numerous boys, and began to experience new and intense body sensations.

In the 1950s, before the Pill, sex without commitment was an anomaly, incomprehensible to my generation's view of the world. A girl in that era cared mightily about how her body appeared to others; however, beneath the surface she must save it, never penetrated, in anticipation of her marriage bed. Her aim was to be a wife and mother—the *sine qua non* of existence, the purpose of her life. That was culture's preordained role for women. As a child of her times, formed by and expressing the religious tenets and moral standards of a patriarchal, puritanical world, she wrapped her body-self tight as a gift for her future husband, her one true love.[12]

After I graduated from high school I wanted to attend college and perhaps (and only perhaps) enjoy a brief premarital career. Marriage was my ultimate goal, and once married, being a wife and mother would be my full-time job, my life's fulfillment. I graduated from college and married at age twenty-two. In marriage I came into my body in a new way. My body, no longer objectified as "a gift," felt safe in the sanctity of vows and commitment. Somewhat inhibited and a bit fearful, I gradually learned the wonders of mutuality, shared sensuality, and passion. And life went on.

The ebbs and flows of relationship shaped my experience for the next twenty years, though the inextricable power of hormones, premenstrual tension, latent career ambitions, bruised egos, and the tedium of familiarity tested the bonds. Through tears, hurt, growth, lust, loss, and renewal I became more fully woman. During this time I started having babies, and my body guided me into a new appreciation of life's natural processes. Although conventional medical practice at the time advocated total anesthesia for a mother to avoid the pain of childbirth, I wanted to be present and awake as my babies came forth from my womb. I wanted to experience this miracle of life to the fullest. I was lucky. My babies came without complication, though in rapid succession, three in three years. In the final moments of their deliveries, after the ordeal of labor (aptly named), I experienced a rare completeness and knew that body/mind/spirit are one—nature/God's miracle manifest in a total, in-the-body, immanent experience. I then had two miscarriages and decided my body was saying our family was complete.

Those next years are a blur of diapers, dinner parties, hospital service, political campaigns, PTA meetings, carpools, husband's professional conventions, family vacations, entertaining clients, camp visitations, Sunday school teaching, vacation Bible school, graduation ceremonies, tennis lessons, graduate school courses, part-time teaching, and more and more. By the time I was forty, I was working outside the home with multiple obligations to family, job, and community and questioning everything—my life's direction, my obligations, my relationship with my children, my relationship to God, the validity of my religion, the justice of my society, and my marriage.

My body responded. During those years intense back pains incapacitated me for days at a time. (I have since learned that a prime location for the accumulation of the neuropeptides generated during prolonged, unrelieved stress is the spinal column.) My body was telling me that my life was out of balance and it was time to learn new ways to restore equanimity and health. I began to listen to the warning signals and committed myself to regular exercise, better nutrition, and the establishment of priorities for the use of my time. I was starting to learn about the deep interconnections of mind and body.

But not until the next decade, when my father died of Alzheimer's after seven years of slow deterioration, did I confront the deep interconnections of body, mind, and spirit. Before that time I just took it for granted that there was a God in heaven who loved me. My father had introduced me to this loving God years before. Every night when I was a little girl, my daddy tucked me into bed, told me a story, and listened to my prayers. Father in heaven and father on earth were inseparable in my young mind. My daddy beside me loved me, so I knew our Father in heaven loved me.

Through those young adult years, as my knowledge of the world increased and my education taught me to think critically, I had come to understand that my childhood concept of God as a bearded grandfather type sitting on a golden throne in the great beyond was a culturally created metaphor. I also was questioning the Christian church's patriarchal bias and becoming increasingly alienated from its traditional theology. I explored multiple interpretations and views within the Christian faith and the different ways other cultures and religions express their experience of the divine. Developmentally, I had come to terms with my childhood attachment to my father and gained a great deal of psychological independence.

Although my notion of God was changed, my belief in a divine loving power, active in the world, held strong. But as my father's body and mind diminished in living death, my faith was shaken. What was happening to my father's soul? What was happening to his life? Where was God?

Two thousand miles separated me from my father, so I did not share the burden of his daily care, which fell to my mother and brothers. But my anguish was constant. In semiannual visits over a period of several years, I watched him lose physical strength and control as his body crumbled into an inert mass, confined first to a wheelchair and then to a bed. Verbal communication, eye contact, and finally personal recognition slipped away. He no longer knew me. On my last visit a couple of months before he died, he gave no indication or acknowledgment of my presence, but he gave me something. He sang hymns from his childhood I never before had heard him sing. At that moment the ineffable soul of my father took me back over seventy years, to a time before his illness he had long forgotten. What a gift. I caught a glimpse of the words and spirit of a young boy that grew to be the father I loved.

My life went on. I functioned in my external world, but my internal world dried up. I went blank. I felt dead. My father's illness destroyed my connection with God. A friend who had lost his wife to cancer recommended I try meditation. He gently led me to still my mind, to quit trying to figure it out, to stop asking questions and looking for answers. He urged me to become aware of life in a very different way, not as active engagement, but through quiet observation of the most basic manifestation of living—my breath traveling in and out of my body. He taught me to meditate. So simple, so difficult, so powerful. Through months of practice and compassionate guidance, I gradually awakened to a new reality, a new understanding of life. By stilling my mind and quietly observing my breath, I slowly came to understand what it means to be present in the moment and connected to the force that permeates all of life, not a transcendent mystical knowing, but a peaceful, grounded awareness. I recalled the words of Paul Tillich that I had read years before, that God is the ground of our very being. God is not out there, in the far beyond, but in the depths of existence.

"That depth is what the word *God* means. And if that word has not much meaning for you, translate it, and speak of the depths of your life, of the source of your being, of your ultimate concern, of what you take seriously without any reservation. Perhaps, in order to do so, you must forget everything traditional that you have learned about God, perhaps even that word itself."[13]

I came to a gradual realization that God is within and without, throughout all creation, not just up there—above and beyond. I learned a different way of knowing God, an assurance of divine presence, not because of petition, good behavior, or reason, but through opening myself to the connection, the spiritual reality, that is within as well as outside my body—a connection to be realized but never explained.

I accepted that I could not know what happened spiritually within my father. I would never know my father's perceptions during his illness. Even before his illness, there were myriad parts, at many levels, of his life I would never know. But I knew we shared much; he had given me much. In our relationship we shared the knowledge of God. I grieved for my daddy and gradually, painfully came to accept his prolonged death as part of his life. In time I would let go of my pain and remember his love, which will always be a part of me.

Within three years death struck another very personal blow. My mother-in-law, a woman I loved deeply, lost physical and mental capacity and died in circumstances very similar to my father's. She had been my female support system, my mentor and guide through my adult years. As a young bride, I moved from California to Tennessee, thousands of miles from family and childhood friends, into what seemed at the time to be foreign territory. Folklore warned me against mothers-in-law, particularly southern steel magnolias. I anticipated a subliminal tug-of-war for her son's affection. Instead, I found a warm, lasting welcome and an unobtrusive support through the highs and lows in the decades to come, until our roles gradually reversed, and it was I who was supporting her.

Again, I faced a profound loss, but something was different. Her death rekindled my passion for living. I felt compelled to try to pass along to others the gifts she had given to me. We all die; that is a part of life. There is much we will never understand or be able to control. But I was learning how thoughts and perceptions shape our reality. Our future is unknown; our past gone; only in the present can we live.

Although my culture defines old age in negative terms, almost exclusively by physical characteristics and medical criteria, I was learning that personal well-being is intrinsically interconnected to an individual's beliefs and attitudes, regardless of age. I experienced how the spirit moves one beyond cultural expectations and values to a new and fuller understanding of the meaning of life in the body of the crone. Not long ago I penned these words:

> Listen, listen
> The clock strikes,
> the sun sets.
> When will I be no more?
> When was I ever more than this moment,
> this breath,
> this instant of reality?
> Sandwiched between the yesterdays and tomorrows
> a span quantitatively scored.
> Though I grow old
> I find comfort in my body.
> Spirit infuses every molecule
> in this matter of being.
> An astounding gift.
> The unique mystery.

PART ONE

AGING THE OLD WAY

2

The Cultural Context

As we . . . enter the twenty-first century, previously unimagined
numbers of people are growing to be very old in America. . . .
—*John L. Rowe and Robert W. Kahn,* Successful Aging

The Demographic Revolution

White hair and powdered wigs were a mark of distinction in colonial
times; today, several centuries later, billions of dollars are expended
annually on hair dye to hide the gray that comes naturally as one ages.
The color people tint their hair reveals a great deal about how our
culture views aging. In the 1700s, when the average life expectancy
was thirty-nine years, the wig-maker, also known in colonial times as
a peruke-maker, was as essential to the well-heeled personage as the
butcher. Old age was venerated in colonial America;[1] today, in a culture
where the total population is rapidly growing older, youth is venerated
and aging is feared.

Assumptions about aging that the young within a population make
may be very different from how an old person perceives his or her own
state, however. The perceptions of the young are based largely on demographic statistics, opinions of the "experts," and media reporting—what
others tell them; the perceptions of the old are based on what they know
firsthand—on lived experience.

Currently we read and hear a great deal about the increasing longevity of individual lives in America and the effect that the astounding
increase in the population of old people has on the U.S. health and
social systems. But little has been reported about how this dramatic
shift in the demographics of the United States impacts the individual, as
he or she approaches and lives beyond the sixth decade of life. According to the U.S. census of 1900, about 4 percent, or approximately 3
million people out of a total population of 76 million, had lived past

their sixty-fifth birthday. In 2005 the population is 291 million people, about four times as large as it was in 1900; the number of individuals sixty-five years or older is nearly 36 million, twelve times what it was in 1900, composing 12.4 percent of the total population. Looking to the future, we see that a huge young-to-middle-aged (between thirty and forty-four years of age) cohort is close to 86 million individuals, approximately 30 percent of the current total population. These people will become sixty-five within the next twenty to thirty years.[2] In thirty years the ratio of workers (under sixty-five years of age) to retirees (over sixty-five) will be 2.6 to 1. Today it is 4.9 workers to 1 retiree.

The following table is a recent breakdown by age of the nation's population, found online at www.census.gov.

U.S.A. Population Statistics in Brief

	1990	2000	2003
Total population (1,000)	248,791	281,423	290,810
Under 5 years old (1,000)	18,765	19,176	19,769
5 to 17 years old (1,000)	45,184	53,119	53,274
18 to 44 years old (1,000)	107,579	112,183	113,143
45 to 64 years old (1,000)	46,178	61,953	68,704
65 years old and over (1,000)	31,084	34,992	35,919

Over 40 percent of the U.S. population in 2003 was clearly middle age—over forty years old. Statisticians reckon that, by simple projections based on current demographic information, by 2030 older adults (over sixty-four years of age) will compose over 21 percent of the total population—a staggering 68 million elderly people. What's more, the growth of the elderly cohort is expanding because the number of years an old person is expected to live is rapidly expanding. In 1930, the life expectancy of a sixty-five-year-old person was 12.2 years; in 2002 a sixty-five-year-old individual's life expectancy was 18.2 years, and if she or he reached seventy-five years, the expectancy was 11.5 more years of life. Centenarians are the fastest-growing segment of the U.S. population. The second fastest-growing is the age group eighty-five plus. Currently, there are about 40,000 centenarians in the United States, or a little more than one centenarian per 10,000 in the population.[3]

This phenomenon is not limited to the United States. International statistics make it abundantly clear that we are living in a worldwide demographic revolution. The elderly population is expanding all around the world. Industrialized nations (for instance, United States, Italy, Germany, Australia, Japan), as well as developing countries (for instance, Venezuela, Thailand, Jordan) are experiencing an increasing number of elders, both numerically and as a percentage of their total population.[4]

Statistics compiled in the *Handbook of Gender Culture and Health* (2000) furnish a dramatic illustration of the aging population of the entire world. (Note that this table differs slightly from the statistics previously listed for the United States, as the percentages are reckoned on the number of individuals in the population over sixty rather than over sixty-five years of age. To younger perceptions there is little difference between sixty and sixty-five, however; they are both generally categorized as old folks.)

Global Aging Demographics

Country	Percentage 60 and Older in 1996	Percentage 60 and Older in 2025
Italy	22.3	33.0
Japan	20.9	32.9
United Kingdom	20.5	28.7
Norway	19.8	28.4
Romania	18.3	23.2
Uruguay	17.3	20.6
Russia	16.7	22.9
United States	16.5	24.6
Canada	16.5	28.1
Australia	16.0	26.6
Ireland	15.2	24.1
Argentina	13.6	16.8
Armenia	11.7	19.3
China, Mainland	9.5	20.3
Turkey	8.2	15.5
Brazil	7.2	15.5
South Africa	6.7	10.4
Mexico	6.5	12.9
India	6.5	12.2
Indonesia	6.3	13.1
Egypt	5.8	10.0
Philippines	5.4	9.7
Honduras	5.1	8.7
Nepal	4.8	6.5
Zimbabwe	4.3	4.9
Nicaragua	4.2	8.1
Uganda	3.7	3.1

This incredible growth of older populations and increased life expectancy around the world results from multiple causes, including decreases in infant mortality rates as well as of maternal mortality rates at childbirth; spectacular reductions in the occurrence of infectious diseases through immunization; impressive advances in successful medical treatment, particularly in the areas of childhood disease and acute illness and trauma; improved medical diagnostic tools; improved nutrition, clean water, and sewage control, plus other vastly improved public health standards. People are living longer because they get a better start, live in a better environment, know more about staying healthy, and have more knowledgeable medical support along the way.

But increased longevity is not the only reason that the demographics of our nation and the planet Earth are undergoing such a dramatic shift. Another factor that greatly influences the demographics of aging is birthrates.

> The demographic forces behind population aging are straightforward. As human societies gained the ability to control disease, death was postponed for more and more people. And the forces that allowed control of disease, particularly economic development, also promoted lowering of the birthrate by lowering the economic value and raising the economic cost of having children. The result was a larger number of survivors moving into the older ages and a smaller number of infants entering the population, which of course resulted in an aging population.[5]

The impact of birthrates is a compelling reason for the substantial rise in the over-sixty-five population particularly in the United States. An unprecedented upswing of live births, following the end of World War II in 1945, created a tidal wave of new babies, popularly known as the baby boom. What is interesting, but without as serious an impact on the demographic charts, is the equally remarkable acute drop in the fertility rates in 1966, characterized as the baby bust. The baby boom is often assumed to be caused by returning American GIs released from military service and eager to move quickly into a normal, peaceful existence. Economists Peter Diamond, David Lindeman, and Howard Young believe that such reasoning is flawed, however. They attribute the cause of the baby boom to the strong economy of the 1950s, juxtaposed with the relatively low material expectations of the parents who were born and raised during the Depression years. They say that this combination made it possible to have one stay-at-home spouse and the resultant large families of the 1950s and early 1960s.[6] Economic prosperity certainly contributes to the general social psyche (the birthrates during the Depression years of the 1930s were lower than they had been in previous decades) and can be considered as one reason for the increase of the fertility rate of the baby-boom era, but (as I will note in my consideration of the overall phenomenon of aging), social cultural patterns are very complex and not easily explained by a single factor such as economics.

Birthrates are a good example of how multiple factors influence the demographics of a nation. During the 1940s and '50s, patriarchal values (to be considered in the next chapter) were deeply embedded in American culture and tacitly influenced the predisposition and behavior of the people. These values were also a major factor in the choice many women made who worked outside the home during the war but, when the war ended, returned to their traditional role as full-time mothers and homemakers. And too, the purely economic explanation is flawed considering that the relative prosperity of the era continued during the years of the baby bust that began in 1966. Economic factors aside, it must be noted that the beginning of the baby bust correlates precisely with the women's liberation movement and the advent of the Pill, an easy, effective method of birth control.

But the increased prosperity of the nation and the astounding technological advances in consumer products that began after World War II did set a new economic standard for the lifestyle and expectations of Americans. Baby boomers and those born in the United States since the middle of the twentieth century became accustomed to new and increased material, technological, and medical advances, which grew to be the expected norm within a very short time. A paid-for retirement became the basic expectation—taken for granted by every working citizen. The financial base for supporting an individual's retirement was guaranteed by the governmental Social Security program enacted in the decade before World War II to provide pensions for retired workers after the age of sixty-five. In the postwar years, retirement funds were increasingly supplemented through private and corporate pension plans.

As we enter the twenty-first century, however, the ever-increasing cost of an individual's retirement, combined with the aging population, is creating a social and political conundrum. Financial concerns about the long-term viability of Social Security, as well as undercapitalized corporate pension programs, severely challenge retirement funding. The age at which retirement payments should begin is being seriously reevaluated. The times and demographics of today are very different from those when Social Security was enacted by Congress in 1935. In its beginnings Social Security was designed to take care of the "old" folks who lived longer than the mortality tables predicted. In 1935 the average life expectancy of the nation was 61.7 years. In 2005 the average life expectancy is 77.2 years. But before attributing all the financial woes for inadequate future funding of Social Security and underfunded private retirement plans to the emerging avalanche of older Americans, it must be realized that the current lack of money and much of the projected shortfall has been created by past and present government and corporate borrowing against Social Security and pension-fund reserves to pay for current programs unrelated to retirement obligations. These extremely complex social and political concerns are, for the most part, beyond the purview of this book. When promised pension checks are not forthcoming, however, not only do employees who are cheated out of their expected entitlements experience deep feelings of betrayal, but this also provokes heightened fears of aging and resentments against the old throughout the general population.

The aged dependency ratio is another statistic often quoted in political discussions of aging. The aged dependency ratio is designed to give a very rough estimate of the size of the older population in comparison with the size of the population that could be expected to pay taxes to support benefits for the older population. This measurement is far from perfect. It does not accurately reflect the picture. When gross statistics are utilized, large numbers of people are overlooked. For example, the calculation of the aged dependency ratio does not account for those over sixty-five who are employed, nor is there any calculation for the large numbers in the fifteen-to-sixty-four age bracket who are unemployed or underemployed.[7] Partial and misleading misinformation about the dependency ratio can lead to concern and unarticulated resentment among the smaller cohorts of the younger generations as they consider what they perceive as the financial burden they will be asked to assume to take care of the old folks. Numbers and statistics do not tell the whole story. Yet the popular media and political pundits perpetuate beliefs and fears about aging based on misperceptions, incomplete information, and false interpretations of statistics.

Discrimination or other feelings against elders would likely never be admitted publicly; in fact, a young person may not recognize that he or she holds any aversion toward old people. However, economist Stephen Levitt's study of a once-popular TV game show named *The Weakest Link* revealed some surprising and relevant findings. The show included eight contestants who competed for a single prize by answering trivia questions. After every round each contestant could vote to eliminate one of the other players. In the first rounds, it benefited the contestants to keep other contestants whom they thought would answer the questions correctly, since money was added to the pot only with correct answers. Toward the end of the game, however, it was in the best interest of the remaining contestants to eliminate someone who likely would answer the trivia question correctly, as elimination of a strong contender would dilute the competition and gain a better chance at the prize for the remaining contestant. A demographic analysis of those eliminated after every round, both in the beginning of the game and toward the end, found that choices were not necessarily based on what would put the contestant in the best position for winning the game, but rather a "taste based discrimination" against elders. Elderly players were eliminated far out of proportion to their skills. On a show where the average age was thirty-four, it seems that the younger contestants simply did not want the older folks around.[8]

The demographic, economic, social, and political issues caused by America's aging population are the backdrop against which the attitudes and behavior toward older people are set. These factors, in turn, influence the attitudes and self-concepts of older individuals. Societal concerns about aging and the subsequent public and corporate policy thereby developed have profound implications for the elderly individual, not only in the economic and social benefits, or lack thereof, but in relational ways—the ways other people in their shared culture think about and treat them. It is essential to remember that the primary point for understanding aging is that it is a very *individual* matter.

The pervasive fear of aging within today's culture, exacerbated by the increasing number of old people, is fed by the many myths and misperceptions. Policy is created and personal decisions made on purely or partially false or misleading premises. Two of the most destructive myths that feed the fears of the old and young alike are (1) that old age is a pathology and (2) that all old people require long-term institutional care. John Rowe and Robert Kahn, in a recent comprehensive study of aging in America, identified other contemporary myths about aging:[9]

- To be old is to be sick.
- You can't teach an old dog new tricks.
- The horse is out of the barn—once deterioration starts, nothing can be done.
- The secret to successful aging is choosing your parents wisely—it's all in the genes.
- The lights may be on, but the voltage is low—creativity stops after a certain age.
- The elderly don't pull their own weight.

And here are some facts that contradict these myths:

- Of the elderly in the United States today, only 5.2 percent are in nursing homes.
- Remember, Queen Victoria learned to speak Russian in her eighties and some folks in yoga classes do their first handstands in their sixties.
- Ellen Langer, a professor of psychology at Harvard who researched elderly Americans for over two decades, found that octogenarians, bedridden for several years, responded to directed exercise, reactivated lost muscular strength, and improved mental acuity.[10] By the time someone reaches middle age, lifestyle rather than genetics is the primary factor in the quality of one's old age.
- The "typical" old person does not exist—Colonel Sanders started Kentucky Fried Chicken when he was sixty-six and Grandma Moses began painting in her eighties.
- There is relatively little decline in productivity with age, and though with age there is some loss of muscular strength and endurance as well as the slowing of reaction time, experience at a task often offsets the losses; in addition, older workers are generally more satisfied with their jobs, are absent less often, and have fewer accidents than younger workers.[11]

I heard a speech recently by a middle-aged civic leader, probably in his mid-forties, pleading for people to support education for young students in our community, an undisputedly worthy cause. But it was his closing remarks that caught my attention; designed to appeal to the self-interest of the audience, his words said much more than he intended. In describing the young boys and girls, he said, "After all, these are the people who will be *taking care of us* in twenty years." There it was,—an assumption based on popular myth. Most people twice his age are doing a credible job of taking care of themselves, but his remark was based on an unquestioned assumption that people over sixty-five need others to care for them. This may have been true a century ago (although it is questionable), but times have changed.

The Individual's Response

The shifts in human thought and technical capacities that have occurred within the single lifetime of an old American are astounding; even more so for the *very* old, who were born at home and transported by horse and buggy as youngsters. Because of experiences in various wars and the continual flow of immigration, these elders (many of whom were immigrants themselves) have been exposed to the world far beyond the nation's borders and have learned the mores and values of other cultures. The almost-too-numerous-to-mention, socioscientific periods that old folks have been catapulted through are amazing—the industrial age, the atomic age, the space age, the microelectronic age, and now the cyberspace age, where people all around the globe are individually connected by the World Wide Web.[12] These rapidly changing political, social, and technological forces have been the larger context for an individual's personal development within the last seventy to one hundred years. Old folks have lived through many transitions. The ability to adapt continually to changed circumstances and relationships at any age is part of their personal journey. But when old people become a statistic or are seen only as a biochemical entity to be analyzed and manipulated, regard for the personal journey of the aging individual is largely ignored. When medical doctors, sociologists, psychologists, and policy makers focus on the abstraction of aging, the reality and significance of the lived experience is lost.

A supreme faith that, with enough time and money, all of life's problems could and would be solved through science was a guiding force in twentieth-century America. Given the astounding scientific and technological advances that vastly improved the nation's standard of living, unquestioned faith in science is understandable. Old age was clearly marked as one of those problems in 1904 when Elie Metchinkoff coined the term *gerontology* as the branch of science that deals with aging and its problems. The specific naming of the problem was the culmination of a cultural shift in how aging was perceived, which began much earlier in Europe, about the time of the Enlightenment when scientists began to position old age as an affliction that could be alleviated through scientific inquiry and treatment. By the early 1900s, erosion of ancient, medieval understandings of aging as a mysterious part of the eternal order of things began giving way to the secular and scientific. "Old age was [finally] removed from its ambiguous place in life's spiritual journey, rationalized and redefined as a scientific problem."[13]

The medicalization and scientific management of aging has robbed old age of the existential quest to find meaning in that phase of living (an issue I discuss in my next chapter). Within the last two decades, however, researchers of adult development and aging are increasingly intrigued with the "paradox of happiness" and the "invulnerable self" in later life, which demonstrate high levels of life satisfaction among the older population.[14] Old people themselves, when asked to do so, paint a very different picture of the latter stages of life than most reports from the social and medical scientists would lead us to envision.

Aging: A Developmental Stage?

In 1976 Gail Sheehy published her best-selling book *Passages*, which introduced Erik Erikson's life-stage theories to a popular audience. Sheehy's work spoke directly to the middle-class, middle-aged, nonacademic American in a new and different language and confirmed what everyone in that particular cohort was already feeling but not understanding. *Midlife crisis* became the rationale and buzzword for the growing pains that most, if not all, of my contemporaries were experiencing.[15]

The assignment of certain behaviors and emotional "growth task" to specific ages was a relatively new concept that began late in the nineteenth century. A number of noted theorists, building on Freud's concepts about childhood psycho-sexual development stages, expanded the concept by creating age categories and characteristics for every stage of life.[16] By the mid-twentieth century, life stages, designated by specific ages, were taken for granted. Recently the basic assumptions delineating stages in adult psychological development are being rigorously questioned, however, the influence of such theories on contemporary cultural beliefs is strong and still holds sway among many. Particularly influential on the work of gerontologists and adult psychologists were Erik Erikson's theories that defined eight distinct development stages in a human life. Each stage, characterized by discrete social as well as physical and mental developmental hurdles, was said to arise during a particular age in the life of an individual. Psychologists, counselors, and educators came to believe that to achieve a successful, well-integrated life a person must successively master the developmental tasks that are rooted in the specific crisis associated with each age. If the designated developmental task was not mastered during the specified age assigned to the particular stage, there were serious personality repercussions. Within each of the eight stages a personal crisis is activated as the individual struggles to integrate the emerging characteristic into his or her personality. If the task is not achieved, a negative trait takes hold of the individual's personality. The three adult stages in Erikson's theory important in the context of adult aging are:

Stage 6: Young Adulthood—Ages 19 to 40—Intimacy vs. Isolation

In this stage, the most important events are love relationships. No matter how successful you are with your work, says Erikson, you are not developmentally complete until you are capable of intimacy. An individual who has not developed a sense of identity usually will fear a committed relationship and may retreat into isolation. Adult individuals can form close relationships and share with others if they have achieved a sense of identity. If not, they will fear commitment, feel isolated, and be unable to depend on anybody in the world.

Stage 7: Middle Adulthood—Ages 40 to 65—Generativity vs. Stagnation

By "generativity" Erikson refers to the adult's ability to look outside oneself and care for others—through parenting, for instance. Erikson suggests that adults need children as much as children need adults, and that this stage reflects the need to create a living legacy. People can solve this dilemma by having and nurturing children, or helping the next generation in other ways. If this crisis is not successfully resolved, the person will remain self-centered and experience stagnation later in life.

Stage 8: Late Adulthood—Ages 65 to Death—Integrity vs. Despair

Old age is a time for reflecting upon one's own life, one's role in the big scheme of things, and seeing it filled with pleasure and satisfaction or disappointments and failures. If the adult has achieved a sense of fulfillment about life and a sense of unity within himself and with others, he will accept death with a sense of integrity. Just as the healthy child will not fear life, says Erikson, the healthy adult will not fear death. If not fulfilled in this way, the individual will despair and fear death.[17]

During the latter part of the twentieth century the life-stage theory was the gospel for understanding adult development. It created a structure for understanding the sometimes terribly disruptive emotions and self-doubts that an individual experiences when going through a life transition. As a scientific theory, which established norms, life-stage theory gave an emotionally stressed individual (or parent dealing with a growing child) a sense of normalcy and assurance in the midst of the stress and anxiety they were encountering, as their known world seemed to fall apart. Although there were ontological questions and psychological pain, the personal turbulence could be viewed as an acknowledged developmental phase. The anxiety experienced was to be expected at that stage in life and was okay; in fact, it was a necessary part of growth. When categorized as *normal* human development, a crisis of transition was seen as part of the necessary long-term healthy personal development of an individual.

The life-stage theory gave great psychological support to those who were meeting a crisis of change they were bound to face. I believe this is the theory's greatest strength, along with identifying that there are developmental tasks that individuals in our society might face, though not necessarily at a prescribed age or in the order delineated. For example, Erikson's stage 5, which occurs during adolescence (ages twelve to eighteen) is marked as the "identity vs. role confusion" crisis. However, such a crisis of identity does not necessarily occur between the ages of twelve and eighteen; I know women who have been emotionally torn apart with that question in their late thirties or sixties. Nor is "integrity vs. despair" confined to late adulthood. Depending on their situation, individuals confront personal developmental tasks at different times during their lifetime. Even so, a benefit of the theory is that it provided a psychological framework for individuals to expect and accept change and transition in their lives that many times lead to personal crises. In today's world creatively dealing with change is one of life's greatest challenges.

Empirical evidence has discredited most of the basic premises of the life-stage theories, both on an individual and societal level. In a postmodern era, life-stage theory is seen as a conservative, middle-class cultural construct that grew out of our Western scientific penchant for classifying phenomenon, seeking norms, and creating predictability over the long term. Today we now understand that age-specific developmental tasks do not describe adult behavior in other places and at other times. In fact, until around the seventeenth century, with the growing impetus to quantify everything, people did not keep track or concern themselves with their own age.[18]

Building on Freudian early-childhood psycho-sexual theories, contemporary culture has almost fully incorporated the assumption that the early experience of the child shapes the subsequent behavior of the adult. The belief in the continuity of human development has not been sustained by empirical studies or by the life stories of individuals, however. Recent research within social psychology strongly suggests that traits and habits acquired during infancy do not seem generally to persist when one's circumstances are altered. Historical and personal events, accidents, luck, unpredictable occurrences, chance—the context in which an individual lives is not only the stage on which human development transpires, it is a primary influence. Yet the variations in the ways humans may develop are virtually limitless. An individual's response to a situation that might determine his or her subsequent life-course is not predetermined, nor can it be predicted.[19]

Though significant, one's culture and circumstance do not determine one's life. Conscious human beings have a capacity of choice. They are active agents in their own lives, their own development, and their own aging. Drawing on insights from Kant, "Human beings have a conception of what they want and what they should do in order to get what they want."[20] The surprising human capacity for change throughout an entire life span is substantiated by stories of personal transformation. The power of personal choice and transformation is highly significant as we consider cultural expectations about aging and the experience of older people.

3

Beyond Patriarchy

Our cultural history is encoded in our bodies.
—*Morris Berman,* Coming to Our Senses: Body and Spirit
in the Hidden History of the West

Traditionally, a woman's life was not her own: she belonged first
to daddy and then to husband. Indeed, she was raised with the
expectation that she would be—literally, body and soul—some-
body else's.

—*Anonymous*

I was probably in my late sixties when I came to the stark realization
that I would never, could never, figure out my life. Life just is. And life
is to be lived, not figured out. It is not ours to control but a gift we
receive in all its wonders and complexity. I know we are connected
deeply and irrevocably to all that is, yet we are also exquisitely a separate entity that experiences the gift of life in a unique and singular
way. But even stranger and more perplexing is that we ourselves are
continually changing, growing, diminishing—a living, self-conscious
process that ultimately defies reductive definition. However, because
we are acutely aware of how the human species, in spite of individual
differences, conforms to patterns of structure and behavior, our very
nature demands that we build theories and myths to explain and control our existence. This is part of our humanness.

Ten years ago when I started a serious study of aging, I focused on
the way our society fears old age and defines it almost exclusively by
biomedical, physical criteria. I learned a great deal about our culture's
history and beliefs, which are shaped by a tradition of patriarchy and
allopathic medicine, as I describe in the next chapter. I also learned, by
talking with older people, a great deal about the human spirit and the
impulse of some aging individuals to defy cultural expectations and live

a full and abundant, though vastly different, life from what they previously lived.

Today's older women live in a distinctly dissimilar culture than the one that shaped their youthful understanding of their place in the world. Sixty years ago they were taught that *little girls were made of sugar and spice and everything nice.* When they became young women, they were to marry, honor their husbands, nurture their children, tend to hearth and home, and live happily ever after. While it is true that some of the women of this generation were sent to college, it is with the tacit understanding that while there, in a seat of higher learning, their main objective was to find a suitable husband. But if they were so unfortunate not to marry, or if once married their husband should meet an early death, they would have an education by which to support themselves.

Even before the 1940s a few educated, emboldened women tried to establish inroads into the male bastions of the intellectual and professional world. Initially they met little success. It was not until World War II, when most of the men left their jobs to serve in the military, that women were allowed, indeed encouraged, to assume responsible positions outside the home. But when the war was over and the flood of male veterans returned to their former occupations, women stepped back into their traditional roles. Little changed—the public realm remained almost exclusively male. That was over fifty years ago, before the feminist explosion of the 1960s that forever changed the world I knew as a little girl.

Yet in spite of the astounding changes within the last fifty years in jobs and opportunities for women outside the home, there is an underlying theme of inherited attitudes and behaviors that countless women still hold, albeit many times subliminally, that place them squarely within the traditions of their culture. The patriarchal belief system, that man is the measure of all things—woman is his helpmate—defined Western civilization. Archaic myths from the beginnings of Western civilization capture these beliefs that sanctioned absolute power and unchecked promiscuity as male privilege and designated women as keepers of the hearth and home. In Greek mythology, lusty-natured Zeus was king of the mount. His wife, Hera, though highly spirited and rebellious (some say because of Zeus's many infidelities within his marital relationship), was kept in her place—minding the palace, subordinate to him. In the Judaic and Christian traditions, God took a rib from the first man, who was put on earth to dominate the flora and fauna of his creation, and created woman as a companion and handmaiden—a helpmate to her man. These are the stories of man and woman that shape the culture into which I was born.

My sole aspiration as a young girl, and as a young woman, was to find a good man, become a faithful wife and devoted mother, and live happily ever after. Never, never did I envision or even think about what would happen in the *ever after*. That was far over the horizon, way beyond my focal point. But here I am, living in the ever after and searching for a script, guidelines, for life at this stage of my development. My *ever after* is shaped by the years I have lived since the *then* of my childhood and the *now* of my life today. These have been extraordinary years for the position and role of women in American society. Women born before the 1940s lived their formative years in a patriarchal world. Their role throughout life was to be one of response and adjustment to, and care for, others. The "sexual revolution" of the 1960s brought seismic cultural shifts that dramatically redefined mores, morals, and perceptions of a woman's place in society. Thus, now, forty years later, younger women live in a far different world from that of their mothers, and many are caught up in a major juggling act of balancing their place in both the public/professional and private arenas. The glass ceiling prohibiting access to the seats of power for women in business, the professions, and public service may not be completely shattered, but there are major cracks. The lives of younger women are very different from those of their mothers. They may no longer believe in the "happily ever after," but another major concern gnaws at their self-perceptions.

Female concerns about growing old are frozen in a society that fears the aging process. Face-lifts, antiwrinkle creams, tummy tucks, and the myriad other antiaging procedures and potions rack in billions of dollars annually. Younger women dread becoming old women. They know, though they don't want to think about it, how their society views old women. It is part of their heritage; it is part of their reality. Before a woman grows into old age, she only knows it from afar and looks at it through the lens of her culture—not a very pretty sight. Becoming an *old* woman is an unwelcome phenomenon. Where do women find guidance for how to live the life of a crone? I recently showed a piece of writing to a good, longtime male friend where I referred to myself as a crone. He cringed and said, "No, you're not. Don't call yourself that." We are a culture in deep denial of natural aging and the reality that women get old.

Confronting Patriarchy

An American woman over sixty-five has lived through remarkable changes in the way culture views her role as a female in society. She has, more than likely, experienced a wrenching metamorphosis in how she views herself. Although she may not have thought much about it as a child, through the years she became increasingly aware of patriarchal attitudes within the institutions and social structures in which she was raised. But what does all this mean to her?

The complex web of mores and beliefs that create the fabric of contemporary society is difficult to unravel. Although in the twenty-first century religious diversity and secularism describe contemporary American culture, one of the most important influences on me and most of my contemporaries during our childhoods and early adult years in the middle of the twentieth century in the United States was the Christian church—a church that through most of its existence promoted and enforced male dominance through its theology, doctrine, and practice. That the Christian church and the Judaic/Christian biblical traditions of the Western world were seated in patriarchal constructs is an undisputed historical fact.

In the pure patriarchy of ancient times a female's social status was determined solely by her connection to her father or husband. Wives and children belonged to the father's tribe or family; birth rights and inheritance were reckoned patrilineally, and women were seen as household chattel, the property of the male head of the household. This social system, which society reinforced through centuries of practice, gave women no independent rights or power of their own. Even today, although the laws of the United States and other Western nations promote and protect equality between the sexes, remnants of patriarchal attitudes are subliminally present in many Christian churches and overtly declared by contemporary fundamentalists and conservative Christians (and Muslims) around the world.[1]

Since the 1960s, however, social activists and academicians have aggressively challenged the inequities, influence, and basis of patriarchal bias of all cultural institutions and the belief systems behind those institutions.[2] Seminarians and cutting-edge theologians delving into church history have discovered that the position of women was much different in early Christianity than that found in contemporary practice. At first, little of this new knowledge filtered down into local congregations, and the average older woman, raised within the traditions of her religion, was unaware of the pervasive influence church doctrine and practice had on her sense of self. But as women became aware of the patriarchal cast of their childhood faith, they were torn. Activists renounced their religion for its patriarchal past and left the church to find new guides for spiritual growth or just gave up on religion altogether. Other women sidestepped or ignored the patriarchal issue as irrelevant in the larger understanding of Christian charity. And there were some committed Christian feminists who labored hard to reach expanded understanding by incorporating new knowledge into a fresh interpretation of their faith. Along the way, these women were both supported and scorned by male counterparts.

At a deeply personal level, when I began to confront the issue of patriarchy, it was the all-male Godhead that gave me the most trouble. I had a secure and loving childhood. The fact that I was female never stood in the way of what I wanted to accomplish in my younger years. In time, however, at the deepest level in my spiritual quest, I became troubled. My church and all I knew spoke of Father, Son, and Holy Ghost. I was woman, and where did I fit in? My bonds to the Presbyterian church and my Scotch/Irish heritage were strong. They were part of my sense of self, the linchpin for my family, which connected me to a community I cherished and an ancestry that I treasured. In my early years I did not trouble myself much with feminist theological musings. I dismissed the church's all-male nomenclature as an archaic remnant from the past and left it to my feminist sisters to work it through. But, in my mid-forties, as my children grew into adulthood and I was no longer engaged in full-time mothering, I began to reassess my role in life and my sense of self. At this point of major transition, I needed spiritual guidance and began paying a great deal more attention to the words and forms of my religion. I did not find what I needed within my church at that time, but rather than actively protest, I silently retreated into myself.

I found and followed a Jungian path inward to explore the depth and breadth of spiritual reality through independent study. I also read a great deal of church history and deeply appreciated the scholarship that was bringing recognition of the feminine into the mainstream of the contemporary Christian quest. My search expanded to the investigation of other religions.[3] The more I searched the more I realized that the root of all faith systems is the core encounter with God as a living, guiding spirit. The horrific problems between peoples come when religious people, in an effort to preserve and spread their faith, claim the exclusive lock on truth.

Jung told a story to describe how the ineffable spirit of the divine is too often lost by established religions. His tale begins when a small group of people discovers a bubbling spring of pure, life-restoring water while wandering in a dark forest. Excited about the spring's miraculous power to refresh and restore their dreary lives, they rush to tell others of their extraordinary find. Many people come desiring to experience the effervescent wonder and are dazzled by the potency of the newly discovered restorative water. As more and more people come, some of them start to meet regularly at the spring. In time, those who gather on a regular basis feel compelled to protect, honor, and explain the water's unassailable power. They develop stories about its ineffable capacities. They pile rocks around the circumference of the spring to protect it from outsiders who might not appreciate its attributes. Within a couple of years they construct a large, intricate edifice to accommodate the hoards of people who are attracted by the stories and the beautiful construction. Now formed in an established congregation, they feel safe in the presence of other like-minded people. They develop elaborate ceremonies to pay tribute to the healing powers of the water and construct systems of governance to assure the perpetuation of the ceremonies and upkeep of the edifice. In fear of losing what they have built, they become suspect of people who do not join with them, who do not believe as they believe. Over time, those who do not join them at the spring become their enemy. So preoccupied with what they have constructed and are protecting, no one notices that the spring has dried up. Jung's tale does not end there, but goes on to describe another small group of people, in a different part of the forest, finding a lovely fresh spring burgeoning forth with life-giving waters.

I came to cherish Jung's insights that the mysteries of the spirit of God, in an ever-changing world, defy absolute definition and categorization. Feminist scholars, who have uncovered patriarchy's suppression of the feminine within interpretations of the nature of God, are finding answers beyond the strictures of the past.[4] They are sorting through the maze of competing theologies, showing that even though the patriarchy of ancient tribes resonates throughout the historical narrative of the Judaic and Christian religions, there is strong evidence in the Old Testament that the feminine goddess of wisdom, Sophia, was revered, not as other or secondary, but as a sublime attribute of Yahweh.

Figurines from the Iron Age, found in recent archaeologist digs are believed to represent the goddess Asherah, wife and coequal of Yahweh, and cause us to reread ancient biblical texts for new insights. Although interpretations vary among scholars, almost all agree that the pre exilic Israelites were not strictly monotheistic, but worshiped Yahweh together with Asherah, as either a feminine dimension of or consort of Yahweh. It was after the exile that the divine feminine disappeared, when the writers of the biblical text sought to consolidate power of the Israelite nation through religious reform and central authority.[5]

The teachings of Jesus and early church history reflect a deep reverence for the divine feminine as well as respect for the equality between the sexes, but by the fourth century the church fathers had replaced Sophia—the ancient symbol of wisdom and up to that time the representation of the feminine in the Godhead—with male designation. The triumvirate of God from that time forward became all male—Father, Son, and Holy Ghost—even though throughout the history of the church theologians and mystics have kept alive traditions of spirituality that explicitly evoked the feminine in God and affirmed the humanity of women. But such voices were often ignored or systematically and even violently suppressed.[6]

The ontological standard of *selfhood* was male, regardless of gender, and patriarchy dominated the Christian church for two thousand years. The accepted belief and practice was that females were created to serve males. A woman's needs and position were defined only through her relationship to a man. A woman knew herself only through approval by or submission to the men in her life. With the loss of the feminine in the symbolic representation of divinity, how could a woman in her deepest spiritual longing know herself as anyone but other? Furthermore, older women were doubly oppressed. Not only was the feminine divine subverted with the loss of Sophia, the crone was destroyed theologically and literally. By the late Middle Ages, old women were the pariahs of the culture—symbolically excluded from the spiritual dimension of life and actively persecuted by the church.

In prepatriarchal cultures the world over, a triple goddess symbol for the divine incorporated the three stages of female existence—virgin, mother, and crone—into one goddess. The old woman was a prominent and indispensable symbol in the ancients' scheme of spiritual understanding. The ancient goddess symbolism inherently and inseparably linked the cyclical representation of nature to the basic understanding of all of reality—material and numinous. The crone, the Indian goddess Kali, the Scottish enchantress Morrigan, and the Celtic Cerridwyn represented absolute, mysterious power to their various cultures. Known as a hag (more about that later), the crone symbolized power over all of life, including death, and was believed to be essential for rebirth in the ongoing cycle of nature. Patriarchal religions with a linear view of reality did not incorporate the cycles of nature within their systems of theology, and any symbolism of the crone was denied. Subsequently, the church fathers systematically destroyed a vital third of feminine reality. The medieval church did all in its power to obliterate any traces of a belief that attributed divine wisdom or power to the feminine and the influence of the crone. The crone became identified as a rapacious, evil destroyer of life, while Mary, the young virgin mother never tainted by natural impregnation or aging, was beatified for her blessings to their patriarchal society. The church held absolute power in medieval Europe, and its Inquisition systematically set out to destroy all witches, that is, all old women.

> The Inquisition's campaign [founded in the 12th century] to cut women off from their own direct experience of spiritual vision, or their Goddess-given moral codes, occupied nearly five centuries of European history. It has been estimated, though the number is in dispute, that 9 million women were executed after 1484, and uncounted numbers before that date.[7]

It is very difficult to step back in time to understand the motivations of men or women in a different culture in a different time, but the persecution of old women is recorded history and still subtly influences the regard for the crone in today's culture.

Etymologies

> It is often forgotten that [dictionaries] are artificial repositories,
> put together well after the languages they define. The roots of
> language are irrational and of a magical *nature.*
>
> —*Jorge Luis Borges*

Words fascinate me. I like to trace a word back to its roots, explore the
etymological grounding of its beginnings, and then follow the tug and
pull of usage, the historical overlay that gradually obscures its original
sense, and many times radically changes its meaning. I was recently
puzzled while reading a classic novel by Joseph Conrad, *Under Western
Eyes,* originally published in 1911, to find a Russian male revolution-
ist (six years before the Russian Revolution) described as a *feminist.* I
could only surmise from the text that at that time and place a "feminist" was one who believed in the superior intuitive and perceptive
powers of women—a far different meaning than the current definition
as one dedicated to the political and social equality of women.

Etymologies, which do not provide definitions but give explana-
tions of what our words meant six hundred or two thousand years
ago, are written to help us understand the meaning of a word in its
past context. Archaeologists with pick and shovel sift through the dirt
and debris under which the artifacts of ancient cultures lie buried;
etymologists with equal persistence plow through volumes of archaic
documents to decipher word meanings from ancient times. The meanings they uncover provide clues to the underlying values and mores of
a distant time and place. We learn a great deal about the history and
values of a culture as we trace the metamorphosis of a word's meaning
back through the centuries. Too often we assume that a word's meaning is a precise, universal unchanging definition found in a standard
dictionary. Not so. What we find in the dictionary is a definition that
conforms to the culture in which the dictionary was written.

What does it mean to be an "old woman"?

Sitting beside my desk is a very helpful book I use four or five times
a day when I am reworking a piece of writing: J. I. Rodale's *Synonym
Finder.* In this trusted source I did not find the term "old woman,"
but found the synonyms for "old womanish": "finicky, hard *or* difficult *or* impossible to please, fussy, persnickety; over-fastidious, prim,

priggish, prudish, hidebound, fuddy-duddy, stiff-necked; spinsterish, old-maidish." Whoa! Those words do not describe the old women I know nor, looking from the inside out, do they square with my own feelings about myself. (In the same source the words defining old man are: "graybeard, old-timer, old boy, elderly man, grandfather, venerable, patriarch . . . senior citizen, golden ager.")

This simple reference tool demonstrates how millenniums of patriarchal attitudes within our culture give shape to the simple meaning of a word found in contemporary, everyday language. One of the synonyms given for old woman is *hag*. I wince when I hear an older woman called a hag and marvel at its current hateful connotation when its original meaning was rooted in the ancient Greek word *hagia*, which meant holy or saintly, as in *Hagia Sophia*. Modern dictionary definitions have completely lost these saintly origins. *Webster's New Universal Unabridged Dictionary* (1996) defines *hag* as "an ugly old woman, especially a vicious or malicious one."[8]

With further investigation we find that even conscientious etymologists are not immune to the influence of their cultural milieu. One of my most prized possessions, which my husband at considerable expense gave me several years ago, is the new and revised edition of W. W. Skeat's *Etymological Dictionary of the English Language*, published in 1901. In this research aid, I found that the Anglo-Saxon root of *hag* is "a prophetess or witch," *witch* and *hag* being synonymous with "an ugly old woman, especially a vicious or malicious one."[9]

These definitions and etymologies tell us much more about the last thousand years of Euro-American culture than about old women. There is some good news. Times are changing. Now, some one hundred years after Skeats published his work, the *Online Etymological Dictionary* (http://www.etymonline.com) lists the origin of the word *hag* as "witch" or "fury," but there is a profound difference. There is no negative connotation in the word *witch*. Rather, this twenty-first-century source says that *hag* in the original meaning (c. 1225) is one of the magic words for which there is no male form, suggesting its original meaning was close to "diviner, soothsayer . . . woman of prophetic and oracular powers . . . village wise woman."

Dipping way back in time, before the dawn of patriarchy, to other epochs and other cultures, we find that old women were believed to have special spiritual capacities. In goddess cultures where the divine was perceived as feminine, to be considered a prophetess or sorceress, a witch or hag, was to be revered. Before the advent of patriarchal Confucianism in 200 B.C.E., the Chinese character *Wu* (later translated as "witch") meant "woman shaman," and a Wu was the revered intermediary between the natural and supernatural world; in the West, until the early Middle Ages before the Inquisition, *hag* meant "sacred knowledge" and witches were seen as healers.[10] Even today, remnants of this original meaning are heard as we find relief by rubbing witch hazel on tattered skin or aching muscles.

As I probe within my own psyche to try to better understand my responses to my life at this stage, I begin to wonder how patriarchy has shaped my sense of self. My roots, both maternal and paternal, reach far back into northern European soil—England, Ireland, Scotland, and Germany; some of my substantially patriarchal base was planted very early in American soil during colonial times. Though I claim much of my heritage from my mother's people, I realize that it is the memories of the males within her lineage that I know best, except for one treasured exception.

In my jewelry box lies a lovely old topaz brooch that I treasure and don on special occasions. It has a remarkable and perhaps mythical history, which begins in Ireland in the early 1600s. Those ancestors with Celtic blood surging through their veins made vocal dissent to the imposition of state religion on their souls. Many generations ago, my forefather, whom I claim with pride, was put in prison for his belief. His wife, a small woman whose height when standing on tiptoe barely reached her husband's chin, devised a scheme to secure his release. She put on many skirts and petticoats and a large brimmed bonnet, topped by a long scarf over her head, and walked to the prison with a freshly baked cake. The jailer must have been a fairly decent sort, for he allowed her to take the cake into her husband's cell. Once there, husband and wife exchanged clothes, and he, with bent knees and stooped shoulders, shuffled past the guard to freedom and caught the next ship to Holland. When the jailer discovered that it was the woman, not the man, locked behind bars, he felt no compunction to hold her (after all, women were of no count) and released her from confinement. She followed her husband to Holland. Once reunited, they secured passage to America where their freedom of religion was assured. He gave her the topaz brooch, which I now hold dear, in esteem and thankfulness for her bravery and indomitable spirit.

Women come alive in stories from the past, but in a male-dominated culture, they needed to perform incredible feats to be recognized and remembered. One woman I interviewed described her frustration in a psychodrama session several years ago, when she was asked to use individuals from the group as models of her family, and to place them on stage in positions that would reflect their relationships to one another. She easily envisioned the relationships between her father and three brothers, but the placement of her mother was difficult. "I saw her in the background; she was there, there all the time, but I can't visualize her in any distinctive role. She was just in the background." This woman's culturally trained psyche saw her mother as the backdrop to the men in her family.

This was my culture. My remembrance of my mother's mother is very weak—my memories of her father, my grandpa, are vivid. In 1945, my mother's father died and her mother, Grandma Robinson, moved from Deming, New Mexico, where she had lived most of her adult life, to Bakersfield, California, to the home of her only daughter. Ours was a modest three-bedroom house, uniquely extended by my father a number of years earlier, when he had the wheels removed from a railroad caboose and moved it into our backyard. The caboose, still with its cupola, the envy of all the neighborhood kids, was modified for a bedroom and bath for my two older brothers, so that when my baby brother was born in 1943, he and I could each have a room of our own in the main house. When Grandma came to town, my older brothers had moved away, and the caboose, with the addition of a small kitchen, became her apartment.

The strangest realization about Grandma's residence with us is that I remember so very little about her. Why is there such a blank space in my recall for the more than ten years she lived with my family? It may have been adolescent self-absorption, when I cared more for my peers than for family. Yet I cannot help but wonder if I was caught up in a subliminal, patriarchal dismissal of old women that was part of my culture, part of my very attitude toward others.

Grandma was there. She took care of my little brother when my mother went out. I am sure she ate meals with us on occasion, but I can't remember her at the table. This is a woman who, I now realize, was younger than I am now when she joined our family, yet I can remember the details of my bedroom wallpaper better than I remember my relationship with my grandmother. She was a quiet person, whom I know my parents treated kindly and with respect, but she and my mother were never emotionally close. My mother, too, was a "daddy's girl."

When my younger brother was in junior high school, no longer needing the babysitting services my grandmother provided, Grandma moved again to live her final years with her sisters in Colorado. Here again, I wonder about questions never to be answered. Could it be that what I assumed was familial loyalty and sense of obligation on my father's part, that of giving a home to his widowed mother-in-law, was in fact a mutual arrangement whereby Grandma maintained a sense of worth in her culturally defined role by helping my mother nurture and raise my little brother? When my brother and mother no longer needed her, she moved on to be with her three sisters who had never married. Oh, the complex web of personal history! It is so very difficult to ferret out those subliminal beliefs we learned in childhood that continue to influence our attitudes today.

Yes, aging is a very personal matter, and the following two stories reflect two different responses to the power of patriarchy on an older woman's self-perception.

Judy's Story

"Vanity is our culture—I don't like to use makeup. We have to paint up and fix up in order to meet men and the public—mainly men."

I had known Judy casually for years. She is outgoing and funny. I always enjoyed exchanging pleasantries with her at neighborhood parties, but until I asked her to talk about her aging body, our conversations were friendly yet superficial. After we talked for a couple of hours, trusting in the anonymity of my interview, she gradually revealed her story.

It began over seventy years ago in a small town in northern Mississippi, where her father owned the dry-goods store and was a pillar in the local Baptist church. Young Judy was a tomboy, much preferring climbing trees and playing baseball to dressing dolls. She remembers her childhood as one of the best times of her life. Even when the other kids teased her about being a fatty, she deflected their barbs with humor and became the schoolyard clown. By the time her weight might have become a problem to her, however, it was not an issue. She said, "My fat fell off when I was fourteen." Her outgoing, joking banter remained. It is with her today. But as her body matured into womanhood, she not only lost her baby fat, she also lost her freedom and her sense of self. Her culture, church, and community dictated her role as a young woman.

"I've always been shoved into some kind of role. I grew up a Baptist—knew the system wasn't right when I was nine years old. I couldn't believe the God I loved, the Jesus that I sang 'Jesus Loves Me' about, would condemn anybody to hellfire and persecution. You couldn't smoke, you couldn't drink. There was very little you could do that was any fun. About all a girl could do was to get pregnant and then get married. If I did something wrong, I was guilty. At times after I was married I would say, 'If I don't feel better than this I would just as soon go with the worms and die.' Then I would say, 'But I can do something about it. I can drink.' I drank to feel better. An alcoholic drinks to feel better, and alcohol is a depressant."

When her two boys started school, Judy wanted to work outside the home, but her husband was against it. His wife belonged at home. He became a successful businessman. She became an alcoholic. He had a heart attack and died at age forty-five. She at age forty-two inherited his business.

"When my husband died, his business was mine, but I wasn't allowed to run it. My business was left in the hands of a bank. I wanted to learn the business, be involved—I always wanted a career. I went back to college and took business courses. Got all A's. Though I went in [to the business] every day at first, I was shoved aside, never given the opportunity. The men from the bank picked a manager, to save the business for my son." At age fifty-eight, Judy had a slight heart attack.

"Women's health has been neglected, women have just never been treated right—medically or any other way. We are second-class citizens. I had a lot of stress, I was very intense, I was a chronic worrier—it built up to a heart attack. I am not saying I blame it on anybody. Myself as a person let this happen to me."

Judy, who felt trapped in the web of patriarchy, suffered from depression and alcoholism most of her adult life. She deeply resented her situation but felt powerless to do anything about it. This heart attack—a messenger from her body? a messenger from God?—made an extraordinary impact on her. She turned her life around.

"Do you believe in transformation? I do, but it sure can be a hard struggle. I tell people I am actually ten years old. My life changed when I had the heart attack—that was when I was fifty-eight, I am now seventy-four."

Since her heart attack, Judy has worked hard at successfully transforming her life, "recovering" from both her alcoholism and the feelings of guilt and inadequacy she feels were instilled in her from the punitive religion and restrictive patriarchal culture of her childhood. Under medical care and counseling she found a medication that helps her maintain psychological balance. She gave up trying to run away from her problems, not through resignation, but through acceptance of what she could not change and a personal commitment to change the things she could. At the top of the list was to quit feeling like a victim. She chose to learn how to focus on what was right in her life. Judy found a course of study that challenged her to recognize and focus on the positive. She came to realize this was her choice. Many of Judy's activities now center on her membership in a liberal, socially active, downtown church, where she feels accepted and respected. She continues to cultivate new friendships, plays tennis two or three times a week, golfs once a week, and exercises daily.

"I have peace of mind. I have found a church where I find joy. And, I have to admit—you don't tell these sorts of things about yourself— the psychologist suggested I take Prozac for my depression. It was just a turnaround. I woke up one morning and felt happy. I then rationalized a lot, trying to think it is not a mood-altering drug, but I now accept I have the same problems. It gave me a new perspective. My miracle drug changed my chemistry.

"It's a combination: Prozac changed the chemistry, the Episcopal church, where I recovered from being a Baptist, gave me spiritual renewal—I am treated marvelously at church, and the philosophy I study shows how to be positive about my life. I like myself."

Judy's story tells of her responses to patriarchy—resentful compliance, unsuccessful rebellion (remember Hera), and alcoholic escapism. As a young and middle-aged adult, she felt her development as an individual was stifled, trapped with no way out. She saw other women entering the business world that she felt was blocked to her, originally from male strictures, but in later years perhaps by her own defeatist attitude and addiction to alcohol. Her body responded to years of stress and frustration. Judy's heart attack was her wake-up call and brought about, with professional help, a serious self-assessment and soul searching and, eventually, spiritual renewal. As she began to peel back the layers of impressed psychological baggage that had rendered her totally victimized by her patriarchal culture, she made a decision that the past, which she could not change, was not going to ruin the rest of her life. She faced her personal pain, accepted herself for who she was, and realized she had a choice. Judy chose, not without a protracted struggle, to become who she is today. She realized that blaming all her problems on the patriarchal attitudes of others was to choose to be a victim. She saw that as long as she felt victimized she would be stuck in her past—angry and helpless. Judy found the faith to drive out the beasts that were killing her. Now as a crone, for the first time since childhood, Judy "likes" herself—a remarkable story of personal transformation.

Amanda's Story

As a young girl in the 1940s, Amanda lived in the rarified environment of Oak Ridge, Tennessee, the atomic frontier where the secret Manhattan Project had gathered scientists and engineers from all over the country to split the atom (a mission unknown at the time to most of the town's 75,000 residents). From her earliest years, Amanda was surrounded by highly sophisticated scientists and technocrats and the environment they created. Educated in the schools of Oak Ridge and in college at the University of Tennessee, with a double major in English and French and minors in European and American history, she became thoroughly steeped in the traditions and culture of Western civilization. After college she changed her last name when she married George, a medical doctor. With a husband and three children, Amanda appeared to the casual observer as a typical, well-educated young matron of mid-twentieth-century America. Yet at the same time, something else was going on. As she quietly developed herself as a poet and writer, she drew deeply from another source, the Appalachian/Cherokee heritage of her maternal grandparents. The wisdom, the stories, the spirit of these people fed her creativity and quickened her sensitivity to the tensions between the two very dissimilar cultures that lay within her soul.

The Cherokees are a matrilineal people. Women were brought into tribal councils and religious ceremonies, and the wisdom of their old women, the grandmothers and aunts, was honored. The word portrait created from my interview with Amanda tells how her roots shape her perception of her body/mind/spirit and gave her strength to break with the patrilineal influences of the dominant culture in which she lived.

I am Amanda. I come from a people of story. My grandfather, a minister, a great judge of stock, started my story. My story forms my relationship to my body.

I am Amanda, born a month early, bottom first—never expose a vulnerability, protect your head—twenty minutes after midnight, during the worst snowstorm in fifty years. I weighed four pounds, six ounces.

Grandfather teased and said I looked like a possum, but pronounced, "She will do well. She has a lusty cry, she likes her dinner, and she has a good head of hair." Strength honored; no comment on beauty.

We are a people of story. Our people's love of story prompts my mother to repeat Grandfather's words every year on the anniversary of my birth. I am thus reaffirmed. My lusty cry signifies the import of power in woman's voice; my hardy appetite promotes strength of body; my blue-black hair proclaims my cherished Cherokee heritage.

I am Amanda. I am one with nature. As a child I liked myself the way I was. My body and I were one—no class or gender distinctions. I ran swift, free, no TV. My people talked not of fitness and diet—their active, self-sufficient lives made them fit and strong.

I am one with nature—rooted in Appalachia. The strength and solitude of the mountains are in my genes. A natural reserve permeates my soul. I honor the way of the deer, reserved, observant, quick, and nonaggressive.

I am Amanda, bearing the creative force of life, the generative wisdom of the grandmothers and aunts. I understand womanhood as both privilege and responsibility—never a curse. Never defined by other.

I am Amanda, one with nature. I am proud of my body—so very happy with my body. Early in life I learned to listen to my body. The body is wise. Just two years ago, wracked with life-threatening cancer and the poisons of chemotherapy, my body held strong. My body did not let me down. I did not lose my immune system. I did not depress.

I am Amanda, one with nature. I find spiritual balance, a balanced interior, balance with God, balance with friends.

Two years ago at the low ebb I withdrew. I could not write. Healing takes energy. Healing is quiet. Nature requires silence to mend its damaged parts. Injured animals retreat to solitude and shelter. Positive, focused energy demands all strength.

The greatest loss was my hair—my Cherokee crown suddenly stripped. Yet the essence of my heritage bred in the bone, stuck, bringing me back to nature's balance. My brain worked with me, playing a continuous loop, over and over and over again—all positive memories of families and friends, all positive forces of my life.

Life force takes many forms. Menopause in woman creates energy to come into one's own. Led by the wisdom and grace of the grandmothers and aunts, older women arrive at the honored "Mother of the Nation" stage of life.

I am Amanda. I have arrived. I celebrate my body. I celebrate my being.

Amanda's experience, though very different from Judy's, clearly marks her journey of what Carl Jung calls individuation—going within to discover the true knowledge of one's self. Through what she calls purposeful thinking, Amanda rejected the power of the dominant culture over her life and found her sense of self within the traditions of her mother's people.

The Challenge of the Crone

We all have a different story. The challenge of the crone is to reflect on that story and make a choice of who she wants to be *today*. A crone's sense of self is the nexus where her conscious being connects with her known world. She may have been defined by patriarchy in the past, but her self-definition today is her choice. The self is not something we are born with, nor something that, once formed, remains immutable; the self is something that is "perpetually created,"[11] never finished. An old woman's sense of self is found in her values and beliefs as she responds and grows in relation to others, to her situation, and to the changing condition of her body, mind, and spirit. Connecting with the spirit in new and different ways is part of the journey of the crone.

4

The Scientific Paradigm

Though the works of reason have lifted innumerable burdens of hunger and sorrow, they have also cast up a new world of power. In that world, some people stand above others in knowledge and authority and in control of the vast institutions that have arisen to manage and finance the rationalized forms of human labor. Modern medicine is one of those extraordinary works of reason.
—*Paul Starr,* The Social Transformation of American Medicine

When a friend my age, in his early seventies, described the rare blood disease found in less than 1 percent of the population for which he now takes a monthly dose of chemotherapy, I asked how it was discovered. "In a blood test after my prostate operation," he told me. I asked if he was in pain or felt bad. His response was negative to both questions. "I am a bit anemic. I'm going to the Mayo Clinic next month for a second opinion on how to treat it." He is worried. His wife is worried. There is an undertone of resentment that his local doctor has not done more.

Ours is a strange age. We are not sure what to think about our bodies or how to treat them. We want health and longevity, freedom from illness and pain, but sure knowledge of how to attain these blessings is not within the purview of most people. The age of scientific discovery has so radically changed the technologies and knowledge of today's world, it is difficult for the average person to feel competent in making decisions about his or her own body. With the constancy of new discoveries and revised interpretations on previous treatments, it is difficult for biomedical professionals to agree on what they should recommend. This is an unsettling dilemma for both patients and physicians.

The spectacular scientific discoveries in biomedicine during the last century have established the professionals in that field as the dominant authority over the course and care of human life in the United States. Although U.S. law clearly states that decisions on medical treatment rest with the individual person, most people, even the well educated, feel incapable of making an informed judgment as to the proper care and treatment of their bodies. Medical decisions, for the most part, are placed in the hands of the experts, those with specialized knowledge and training.

From a long-term historical perspective this authority of bio-medicine is a recent development. Today's orthodox medical practice is based on assumptions established in the seventeenth century when scientific inquiry, breaking away from the ontology of medieval religion, believed that all of nature would be explained by careful, objective observation of the physical universe. Supreme faith was placed in the power of human reason to explicate the observations. In 1641, René Descartes, the premier progenitor of modern Western philosophy, wrote in his *Meditations*, "There is a great difference between mind and body, inasmuch as body is by nature always divisible, and the mind is entirely indivisible."[1] That short phrase, "the body is by nature always divisible," had profound implications for the development of medical science and, subsequently, how old age is viewed in today's world. The belief that the physical body, completely separate from the numinous mind and spirit, is a divisible, mechanical object that must be reductively examined to be understood, became the fundamental premise, the epistemological foundation, of modern medicine. It became accepted fact that disease would be conquered through the dissection and isolation of discrete biochemical bacterial and cellular activity. This is the construct of knowledge in which modern medicine developed and made life-changing discoveries about the nature and treatment of disease. The reductive epistemology of biomedicine shapes the education and practice of biomedical professionals today. As mentioned before, however, it was not until the twentieth century that this reductive medical construct of human life achieved the commanding status it holds in today's culture—a construct that promotes a near-morbid preoccupation with the body's biological systems and its unarticulated counterpart, a pervasive fear of aging.

Although documentation is spotty, historical and anthropological studies show great variation in theories and attitudes about old age throughout human existence. Views on the physiological aspects of aging and the social treatment of old people usually tell more about the mores and mind-set of a culture than about aging and old age itself.

In some primitive or traditional societies, the old, so close to death (less than 3 percent of a population reached the age of sixty-five), were seen as intercessors to the world beyond and were considered to have magical or supernatural powers. However, although the mythical traditions of many cultures honor the elderly and imply great esteem for their wisdom, it has been found that myth and social practice often were very different. The Ojibway in northern Canada venerated old age as long as it was accompanied by good health, but had no tolerance for the infirmed old, whom they routinely discarded. Other primitive tribes, such as the Yakuts of northeastern Siberia, the Ainu of Japan, the Siriono of the Bolivian Forest, the Thonga of South Africa, and the Crow and Hopi of North America, treated the weak and elderly cruelly and abandoned them when they could no longer contribute to the well-being of the community.[2]

Although ethnological data indicate that many of the primitive cultures disposed of their elderly when they lost their faculties, became a burden to the community, or were no longer capable of participating in tribal affairs, there are numerous examples of primitives the world over who honored and cared for their old. The Yaghan of Tierra del Fuego, an extremely poor and primitive people, the Lepcha of the Himalayas, and the Aleuts of the Aleutian Islands were among the tribes who dignified and gave caring attention to their older members. The Arandas of the Australian forest and Zande of the Sudan went even further, equating "graying" men's knowledge with the possession of magic power. In the North American Southwest the matrilineal Navajo also raised the elderly to the sacred plane and credited them with supernatural powers.[3]

In the Cherokee mythical tradition, when it was time for the very old grandmother Selu to die, she went to bed leaving explicit instructions for how she should be buried so that corn, the life-giving sustenance of her people, would sprout forth from her grave.[4] Her death brought continuing life to her people and gave voice to the cyclical view of time and nature. For many tribes and nations of antiquity, "Death feasts are a kind of rebirth for the whole tribe, a rejuvenation of the vital principle. The passage of time is not looked upon as something that brings the future closer but rather as something that thrusts youth back into the past . . . [and through rites and ceremonies] the vigor of a youth is perpetually renewed."[5] The cyclical patterns of nature were continually honored.

When we turn to the recorded history of Western civilization (which primarily references men) we find that Hippocrates, the father of medicine (470–410 B.C.E.), believed that old age, which was considered to begin at age fifty-six, was caused by an upset in the balance of the four body humors (blood, phlegm, choler, and black choler). Comparing the stages of human life to nature's four seasons, he equated old age with winter, advised moderation at this stage, but said that old men should not give up their occupations.[6]

Aristotle (384–322 B.C.E.) is deemed to be the first philosopher to do organized observation and systematic investigations of the natural material world. He believed that all living things had vitality, a soul, and that "the soul being [is] that which gives the form or actuality in living things."[7] Aristotle also believed that life could not exist without heat and that old age was caused by a loss of heat in the heart, where the soul resides.[8]

Although the Old Testament gives every indication that the ancient Hebrews venerated old age, Ecclesiastes 12 (c. 300 B.C.E.), the lyrical lament on the folly of life, renders old age a time of misfortune and darkness. In the second century C.E., Galen of Pergamum (130–203), who looked upon the body as the material instrument of the soul, wrote an all-embracing synthesis of classical medicine that became the unchallenged medical authority in Western civilization for over a thousand years. Observing that the physiological functions of old men were reduced and weakened, Galen believed that old age was something lying between illness and health that was not exactly a pathology. He outlined a specific regime for old men (hot baths, wine, activity, and a detailed diet). It was Roger Bacon (1214–1294), with his passion for experimentation and alchemy, who was one of the first in his time to look upon old age as a disease.

During the Renaissance new theories of aging, reflecting new worldviews, were created. The Swiss teaching physician Paracelsus (1493–1541) believed that the body was a chemical system and that every disease was highly specific in nature and required a specific chemical for its cure. A zealous alchemist dedicated to freeing medicine from its medieval strictures (as Martin Luther, whom he greatly admired, had done in religion), Paracelsus lectured in his native German instead of the traditional Latin of the scholars and burnt the books of Galen, just as Luther had set fire to the Papal Bull. He believed that old age was a process of auto-intoxication as the body's natural chemicals failed to maintain balance.[9]

By the seventeenth century, René Descartes's theory that the body was "a machine made by the hands of God, which is incomparably better arranged, and adequate to movements more admirable than is any machine of human invention" greatly influenced medical speculation. Giovanni Alfonso Borelli (1608–1679), an Italian mathematician and astronomer of note, coupled geometry and physiology in a way indicated by Galileo Galilei and Pierre Gassendi as well as Descartes.[10] He introduced the idea that the body is a machine that gradually wears out. Almost concurrently a German physician, George Ernst Stahl (1660–1734), took an entirely opposite view and "held that the word *machine* expressed exactly what the animal body was not."[11] According to Stahl, living bodies were not governed by the physical laws of mechanics but by laws of a wholly different ilk—the laws of the sensitive soul. He saw chemical processes as the immediate instruments, the natural slaves and vital part of the sensitive soul. He rejected a purely materialistic view of life and held that the weakening of the vital functions caused old age. Vitalism, the name given to Stahl's theory, in the final analysis is not dissimilar to Aristotle's understanding of living entities kept alive by the inner heat of the soul.

By the mid-eighteenth century, old age was more sharply defined in pathological terms as details of the body's deteriorating systems were revealed through postmortem research. It was during this era that a chronological record of the specific age for disease onset began to be kept. These studies provided the necessary information to nineteenth-century scientists for the pursuit of the laws of normality and pathology as applied to senescence (deterioration in old age). The search for both biological and sociological norms was the impetus that led to the birth of gerontology and the social management of aging.

The Establishment of Medical Authority

For most of the last century, scientific knowledge has held a privileged status in the hierarchy of belief. Even among the sciences, medicine occupies a special position. Its practitioners come into direct and intimate contact with people in their daily lives; they are present at the critical transitional moments of existence. They serve as intermediaries between science and private experience, interpreting personal troubles in the abstract language of scientific knowledge.[12]

One of the earliest successes in the practical application of medical science was in public hygiene. The key scientific breakthroughs in bacteriology came in the 1860s and 1870s in the work of Louis Pasteur and Robert Koch. During the 1880s their discoveries were extended and diffused, and by 1890 their impact began to be felt. Isolation of the organisms responsible for the major infectious diseases led public-health officials to shift from the older, relatively inefficient measures against disease to more focused measures against specific diseases. These new efforts made a marked difference in the control of water-borne and food-borne diseases. Sand filtration of the water supply, introduced in the 1890s, was far more effective in preventing typhoid than were earlier methods; required pasteurization of the milk supply dramatically cut infant mortality. With these initial successes, specific chemical and bacteriological tests for disease emerged rapidly at the turn of the century. In the 1880s, the organisms responsible for tuberculosis, cholera, typhoid, and diphtheria were isolated, and by the mid-1890s laboratory tests had been introduced to detect these diseases. "The spirochete that causes syphilis was identified in 1905 and the Wasserman test for syphilis was introduced in 1906. Also the nineteenth century saw advances in the analysis of the urine and the blood that gave physicians additional diagnostic tools for such diseases as diabetes."[13] These seemingly miraculous diagnostic tools were to be extensively employed in the twentieth century.

Such scientific discoveries had tremendous impact on the public's perceptions as well as its health. As technology and biochemistry altered tools and methods of diagnosis, the individual layperson felt incapable of making any decisions about his or her own medical care or, even more significant, how to detect latent disease within his or her own body. Doctors saw the change in their own lifetimes. "Our work in the past ten years has changed tremendously," commented a Minnesota physician in 1923. "Ten years ago no parent brought a child to the physician for examination to make sure that nothing was wrong. Today, I venture to say that the greatest part of the work a pediatrician has is in preventive medicine." The same was true of older patients: "A man comes to the doctor and tells him he wants to be examined, and to be told what to do to increase his span of life."[14]

Scientific allopathic medicine (the treatment of disease by conventional means, i.e., with drugs having effects opposite to the symptoms) treats the body as a complex machine—a complicated, complex, conglomerate of bones, tissues, and organs. This approach to medical education and practice became established orthodoxy in the United States. Pathology was an indication of an invasion or aberration in normal body function. Only through a competent expert's reductive examination, dissection, and microscopic analysis could disease be diagnosed and treated. With this paradigm of understanding the status of scientific medicine assumed near-absolute authority over the ordinary person's perception and treatment of his or her body. Biomedical professionals stood above all others in possession of venerated knowledge and sophisticated techniques that would cure human illness. Scientific authority not only altered private beliefs and behavior, it shaped public policy. To protect individual citizens from quackery and charlatans selling questionable patented medicines, state legislatures passed laws requiring certification from a reputable institution for medical licensure.

These requirements promoted improved standards for all medical education, which at the time was deemed terribly deficient. In calling for reform at his own institution in 1871, Charles William Eliot, president of Harvard University, proclaimed that "The ignorance and general incompetency of the average graduate of American Medical Schools, at the time when he receives the degree which turns him loose upon the community, is something horrible to contemplate, . . . The whole system of medical education in this country needs thorough reformation."[15]

Under the aegis and direction of the American Medical Association, medical education was elevated and standardized. The entrance prerequisites for medical school were stiffened, curriculum strengthened, and requirements for graduation made far more rigorous. Research, along with training, became a primary focus for medical schools. Once graduated, the medical doctor assumed a privileged position in the community. A physician's prescription was required for the dispensing of drugs. To assure the doctors access to the most up-to-date equipment, medical practice shifted from home visits to the hospital.

As scientific knowledge expanded, medical specialization flourished. One specialization, which had tremendous implications for our society's current assumptions about old age, was founded in the beginning of the twentieth century when a group of medical doctors gathered together to focus their expertise exclusively on the problems of human aging. They explicitly identified old age as a major problem and a specific topic for scientific inquiry. In 1904 Elie Metchnikoff formalized their efforts by coining the term *gerontology* as the branch of science that deals with aging and its problems. In 1909 the study of disease and pathology in the elderly was named *geriatrics* by I. L. Nascher. These well-motivated, scientifically trained founders of modern gerontology and geriatrics, along with other scientists of their time, believed that science was a pure exercise of reason—a free realm of inquiry (of the physical nature of the body) that was neatly separated from cultural perceptions and values. This assumption created the framework for aging to be categorized as a life-threatening pathology, an assumption that still prevails in the scientific study of aging.[16] Aging became, and still is, one of many pathologies that science would conquer. The official slogan of the American Academy of Antiaging Medicine, a new medical sub-specialty a group of physicians and scientists founded in 1993, reads as follows: *Aging is not inevitable! The war on aging has begun!*

A massive industry grew up around the privileged position of biomedicine in the twentieth century, and often the medical professionals themselves, believing in the infallibility of their scientific methods, adopted measures (such as using arcane language that disguised meaning and writing illegible prescriptions in Latin) to demonstrate their superiority to those they were treating. A physician's time was of supreme value, and little consideration was given to the hours spent in crowded waiting rooms by patients intent on gaining access to his or her esoteric knowledge. To assure the most efficient use of a doctor's precious time, little effort was made to schedule office visits realistically. (Some physicians scheduled eight to ten appointments within one hour, with full knowledge that only three or four patients could be seen during that time.)

Mortality is the enemy of the allopathic scientist dedicated to the all-out fight to find *the cure*. David Morris, in his book *Illness and Culture in the Postmodern Age*, observes that a

> good index to the character and limitations of biomedicine is what happens when the hope of cure is gone. When all their vigorous invasive procedures prove futile, when the patient can

no longer sustain either the curative assault of medicine or the punishment of illness, the cardiologist and the nephrologist and other specialists are suddenly and curiously absent—not even a courtesy visit is paid. . . . Every specialist who is any good is fascinated with pathology. When faced by the certainty of his own impotence to treat it, the would-be healer too often turns away. If a riddle is by its nature insoluble, it cannot long hold the interest of any but a tiny fraction of the doctors who treat specific organ systems and disease categories.[17]

The vast campaign to conquer disease (and aging is included as such) assumes that the cause of all illness is discoverable and that disease and aging will ultimately be eliminated through the application of science. Both morbidity and mortality will eventually be controlled by understanding and manipulating the discrete particles of living matter of which the body is composed. The more accurately the components of microbiology and chemistry are identified and understood, the more effective the control will be of any disabling process. Illness and aging are considered to be curable. With enough patience, effort, and money, a cure will be found. Geneticist Aubrey D. N. J. de Grey of the University of Cambridge, posits that if the logical, scientific course is pursued, humans will live to be five thousand years old by the 2100s.[18]

Allopathic medicine's focus was the dominant paradigm of twentieth-century medicine and profoundly influenced the physician's treatment of patients and the perceptions of those they treated. Michael Foucault beautifully captures the vaunted status of the medical doctor in his description of the *clinical gaze*. Foucault uses the term to describe the myth of medical infallibility that grew within our culture in the twentieth century. People came to believe that the physician could penetrate illusion and see through to the underlying reality within their bodies. With the clinical gaze the physician had the power to see hidden truth unavailable to others. The doctor with this clinical gaze could diagnose problems, design solutions, and speak about all things wisely. There was no way for anyone to challenge his experience. It just was: only the doctor could tell us the truth and what to do about it.[19]

Sander Gilman, drawing on the insights of Foucault, sagely remarked that "medicine's peculiar power lies not only in its status as science but in the overt helplessness of the individual in the face of illness or in the face of being labeled ill."[20] The power implicit in the physician and the medical setting easily reduces one to a state of passive and dependent helplessness.

> Patients suffering from cancer in the modern era [run] a risk of feeling implicitly de-spiritualized, reduced by their disease to mere matter, at the mercy of renegade cells reproducing nonstop like a runaway production line. In a process that biomedicine only augments with its focus on cells and organs, the tumor in effect replaces the person, the person in effect becomes the tumor.[21]

From this perspective, then, a person becomes his or her illness, and when aging is defined as illness, men and women tend to turn over the care of their bodies to the experts on the underlying assumption that eventually a discovery will be found that will keep them young forever. With ever-expanding scientific knowledge and the creditable success of medical treatment over the last century, this attitude is understandable. After all, the expected life span of an individual by the end of the twentieth century was three times greater than it was in Descartes's seventeenth century.

The Worried Well

Yet one of the phenomena of contemporary medical knowledge is the continual, unsettling change—for example, the downgrading or suspension of a previously prescribed procedure or drug, uncertainty about the ultimate effect or side effect of a particular medical recommendation, disagreement among biomedical experts. For instance, new research finds that the common extra step of removing ovaries during uterine surgery seems to do no good and might increase the chance of dying from heart disease. The removal of ovaries has long been accepted surgical practice, despite little evidence to warrant the procedure. Some 615,000 hysterectomies are performed every year in the United States, 90 percent of them for noncancerous reasons. More than half of the women undergoing a hysterectomy have their ovaries removed as a protective measure against developing ovarian cancer in the future. With these new findings these women now live with the fear of an "early death" from heart disease.

Not only do recommendations and prescriptions for treatment of illness continually change, the very definition of what constitutes illness has changed dramatically within the last decades. Dartmouth Medical School researchers estimate that during the 1990s, tens of millions more Americans were classified as having hypertension, high cholesterol, diabetes, or obesity simply because the definitions of the diseases were changed. Before 1997 the blood sugar count for a diagnosis of diabetes was 140 or more; today it is 126 or more. In that same year the definition of hypertension (high blood pressure) was changed from 160/100 to 140/90. In 1998 the definition for high cholesterol changed from a level of 240 or more to 200 or more; and the body mass index for determining overweight status became 25 or more, changed from 27 or more.[22] Today, three of every four Americans technically have at least one of those diseases. But millions of them are not truly sick and many may never be, even without medication. The Dartmouth researchers said it was unknown whether those people would benefit from early detection and treatment, and it is "an open question" if branding them diseased and feeding them drugs may be causing significant physical or psychological harm. The medical profession's term for these people is "the worried well."[23]

As we enter the twenty-first century, however, we are beginning to see major cracks in the authority of allopathic medicine. Public demands and expectations of the medical professionals are impossible to meet. One dilemma is that even when there is competing information as to the best procedure or drug to treat an illness, the admission by professionals that they "don't know" erodes the confidence upon which the patient relies. One's doctor is "supposed to know," but the law continues to clarify that in the final analysis the individual must decide. At an earlier time the law generally stipulated that because declaring all possible risks would only create unwarranted fears and confusion for the patient, the treating physician was empowered to decide what he or she thought the patient should know. When something went wrong, however, a risk of which the patient was not informed, the courts many times held the physician responsible. State laws have gradually changed over the last several decades to instruct treating doctors that rather than the physician deciding what the patient should know, he or she must inform the patient of the risks that a "reasonable person" would want to know. With the ever-increasing threat of malpractice lawsuits, the current practice is for the doctor to obtain the signature of the patient on a written form that lists all conceivable risks before proceeding with treatment.

This, however, does not remove the threat of malpractice. When something goes wrong and the "cure" does not work, the patient often believes it must be the doctor's fault. And many times it is. It is estimated that there are over 100,000 avoidable deaths annually in the United States due to physician error.[24] Malpractice litigation is major business in today's world. The continual threat of malpractice for both doctors and hospitals creates greater caution and more expensive tests that do not necessarily improve medical care but pervasively reinforce the patient's reliance on the "unfathomable miracles" of modern medicine. The conundrum is particularly evident in the definitions and treatment of aging in the United States.

The Scientific Definition of Aging

With the ascendancy of allopathic medicine that defines aging as a pathology, the growth of an industry centered on aging became a gargantuan force in the American social/political economy. This institutionalization of aging,[25] according to Thomas Cole, created a prodigious change in the worldview of the United States. In his book *The Journey of Life: A Cultural History of Aging in America,* Cole records how aging was constructed over the last century as a medical and social problem to be solved by the professional expertise of medicine, social service, education, and business. "Physicians in the United States joined welfare workers and social scientists in constructing a vision of old age as a clinically distinct phase of life requiring special professional attention and care."[26] The growth of an industry concerned with the needs of an aging population *institutionalized* a stage of life. In using this term *institutionalized,* Cole is not suggesting that most of the elderly in the United States reside in institutions, a popular belief that is not based in reality. Only 3 to 5 percent of people living in the United States between the ages of sixty-five and seventy-four need help with any activities of daily living; by age eighty-five and over, no more than 25 percent need help bathing, and no more than 15 percent need help with light housework and preparing meals. In general, it can be said that severe disability is uncommon among older people.[27] But attitudes about aging are tacitly structured (institutionalized) within our culture and accepted by both young and old as fundamental in their meaning. Traditional medical and social caregivers, who see old age as a pathology and/or social problem, operate with a "rescue" mentality that tends to create a culture of dependency as it undermines the self-confidence of the older individual.

The economic, political, and moral power of the "aging industry" is a very visible part of the contemporary cultural milieu in which individuals function, and is an ever-present component of their aging experience. Both the medicalization and institutionalization of aging fosters fears about getting old and negative attitudes toward old people that, in turn, encourage society to push the elderly aside. Those eligible for retirement, chronologically defined as past sixty-five years of age, are not only socially singled out in U.S. culture, they are conspicuously absent from general social and professional involvement.

On reaching a certain age, one is typically no longer in the mainstream of society. One is set apart as a type and is seen and treated differently.[28] Assumptions about aging are built on assumed "truths" and are continually reinforced through popular media's glorification of youth. This gives rise to the secondary cultural phenomenon of ageism—a cultural devaluation of advanced aging. The experience or value of the individual is lost when "being old" is defined through stereotypes, pathology, and societal myths.

Not only does society set old people apart, but many old individuals themselves pull away from active intergenerational interaction. Granted, some age segregation is the result of a desire of the elderly to be with people like themselves, with a compatible energy level and similar experiences and cultural reference points. People enjoy reminiscing together about a simpler time—walking two miles to school, riding bikes all over town, listening to radio serials, and collecting milk-bottle tops. If one was born in the 1930s and grew up during WWII in a pretelevision era, then one recalls sugar rationing, defense stamps, *Terry and the Pirates*, Jack Benny, Lana Turner, Van Johnson, the jitterbug, Edward R. Murrow, and V for Victory. If born a decade later, the Beatles, the Vietnam War, rock 'n' roll, *Leave It to Beaver,* and *I Love Lucy* are the touchstones of connection.

Even so, much age segregation is culturally structured. The old often respond to being culturally labeled as incompetent by withdrawing from active engagement. When old age is seen as a problem, with its solution placed in the hands of the "professional experts," regardless of how well motivated and caring they may be, the implication is that old people cannot take responsibility for themselves. Our culture tacitly says to the old: *You should no longer have authority over your own life. You, aged one, are a problem that we are trying to solve through the latest scientific methods.*

Cultural messages received by an individual over a lifetime of exposure become imbedded in an individual's belief system and in time become part of that individual's neurological response system. In the contemporary U.S. culture, which values independence and individual responsibility as almost a moral imperative, this message can destroy an individual's self-esteem and sense of self and lead to a depressed state of mind. In this state one loses a zest for living and the simplest personal tasks become monumentally difficult to perform. When one's sense of self is lost, a personal void is created and a nagging question becomes, What does it matter what I do? How do *I* matter? A person's value within our culture is traditionally determined by his or her productivity or service. When an individual is no longer productive or providing service where does he or she find meaning?

When identity is largely derived by measuring oneself against generalized cultural and societal expectations or norms, real problems arise. On the one hand, it is very hard to like oneself when defined as a societal problem; on the other, it may lead to a denial of reality, where an aging person psychologically denies identification with his or her age cohort. William Sadler remembers trying to persuade his father, "suffering from too much empty time in his seventies, to join a senior-citizens club. 'No way, they're too old,' he kept saying, even though [Sadler] pointed out that most were ten years younger than [his father]. The stereotype of aging embedded in his neurons shaped his attitude and contributed to his decline and eventual placement in a nursing home, where he spent eight years of prolonged dying."[29]

Recent studies show that intimate companionship and good friends are very important for successful aging and that socialization is a very effective antidote for depression.[30] It is difficult to make or even maintain good friends when one does not like oneself, however. Depressed people, young or old, tend to withdraw from other people and become isolated. Our cultural institutionalization of aging has not only created a separation of the ages; at a personal level it has created a two-edged sword against the old, undermining self-esteem and discouraging socialization.

From a biomedical perspective, it is true that there are often many debilitating tendencies present with aging, such as high blood pressure, hardening of the arteries, weakened immune system, arthritic collagen accumulation, and loss of short-term memory, but the causes for these debilities are not clearly understood and not all old people have them. Again, referring to controlled, longitudinal research, the "typical" older adult does not exist. Aging is an individual experience; people differ not only in their attributes and behaviors but also in the way they change over time. The results of hundreds of experiments and research projects using both human and animal subjects have shown that chronological age is not a good predictor of function or performance for an individual. Aging is a highly personal process.[31] As noted before, attitudes, beliefs, and mood are the most important factor in health maintenance of the aging.[32]

To consider aging an illness to be cured is a twentieth-century phenomenon grounded in the successes and subsequent pervasive sway of reductive science. It is interesting to note that consideration of chronological age as a factor in human aging is also a fairly recent development. People did not keep track or know their own age until around the seventeenth century, when the growing impetus to quantify and find norms for everything became important. Most of the historical records of Western civilization, based on extant philosophical writings from past civilizations, indicate human life was characterized in three or four ages that denoted the rise and fall of physical power—growth, maturity, stasis, and decline. As best we can tell, there seems always to have been some ambivalence about old age. In the writings of the Old Testament, Plato, and Cicero, however, homage is given to the elders for their wisdom, and when we trace the etymology of the word *old* in Old English manuscripts, *eald* meant trustworthy and venerable. The Indo-European, Gothic, Old Norse, and Old English roots of the word mean to nourish—something old means fully nourished, grown-up, matured—whereas today, with contemporary usage, *old* has a quantitative—number of years—connotation.[33]

There is some good news, however. A paradigmatic shift is occurring. The over-sixty-five cohort of the population is growing rapidly and a new view of aging, though not universally recognized, is emerging. People are living longer, healthier lives, which can be attributed in large part to science and the vastly improved public health standards previously mentioned. With people living longer, there is a growing awareness of the importance of lifestyle, exercise, and nutrition on the quality of an individual's life as she or he ages. The baby boomers, born after World War II in the late 1940s through the early 1960s, are eager to redefine old age as they approach the other side of what was once called "middle age." As demonstrated in chapter 2, the large numbers of this cohort exert a tremendous influence on the culture. John Rowe and Robert Kahn, who study aging in America under the auspices of the McArthur Foundation, observe that "as we . . . enter the twenty-first century, previously unimagined numbers of people are growing to be very old in America. . . . the dynamic changes within the aging population itself, represent perhaps the most dramatic change in American society in this century."[34]

Rowe and Kahn, after ten years of study, concluded that successful aging in the United States today, contrary to popular assumptions, is much more dependent on one's lifestyle and attitude—behavior and beliefs— than on genetic predisposition. Their research shows (though the popular press would lead us to believe otherwise) that the influence of genetics shrinks proportionately as one gets older, while social and physical habits become increasingly integral to one's health—both mental and physical. Even from a purely biomedical perspective focused on pathology alone, research finds a healthy lifestyle and positive attitude prevent or greatly postpone the emergence of morbidity and the onset of chronic disease.[35]

Today we are beginning to understand that the traditional bio-medical focus, which centers on a particular problem in the physical body without consideration of a larger biochemical, psychosocial con-text, is not only limited but destructive. Carl Jung once wrote, "It is not only possible but fairly probable, even, that psyche and matter are two different aspects of one and the same thing."[36] It seems almost ironic that, if we go back into the history of the scientific tradition, we find that Aristotle, the reputed founder of Western scientific epistemology, observed that "when the parts of the body and its humors are not in harmony, the mind is unbalanced and melancholy ensues; on the other hand, a quiet and happy mind makes the whole body healthy."[37]

This is an essential insight for understanding aging. Aging is not a pathology—a compounding of chronic disease. Aging is a living pro-cess that must be understood from both inside (the body/mind/spirit) and outside (within a cultural context), with the realization that there is no clear dividing line between the two. The interworkings are ongo-ing and extraordinarily complex.

A Look at Aging from the Inside Out

To quote the iconoclastic physicist David Bohm, "The great strength of science is that it is rooted in actual experience; the great weakness of contemporary science is that it admits only certain types of experience as legitimate."[38] If attitude is key to understanding the aging process, it is very important to know what shapes the attitudes of an older person. Scientific expertise and its search for norms to define aging do not give a whole and true picture.

Looking beyond medical, chronological, and physical factors, gerontologists during the last several decades have increasingly recognized the power of society and culture in the aging process. However, even here exists the danger of attributing the "problems of aging" to a single issue, forgetting tremendous individual differences and preferences. Understanding aging is extremely complex. Social gerontology must avoid an "oversocialized" conception of humanity. A person is both more and less than a collection of social roles, a seeker of acceptance by others, and a follower of social norms and expectations. On the other hand, contemporary psychology must avoid an "overpsychologized" conception of human nature that sees individuals as cognitive processors, operating independently of their ties to the social world, including family, neighborhood, community, and culture.[39] Individuals have problems and challenges throughout life. Old age is no different.

Only by talking and listening to those who experience old age will we discover the realities beyond theories and scientific norms. Although our dominant culture fears aging and sends a strong antiaging message, a different theme is found many times within the experience of the elderly. As an example, we can turn to the narrative of an eighty-year-old woman whose early ambitions to be a medical doctor were thwarted. She has confidence in the biomedical paradigm, but through her own experience she has learned that it does not hold all the answers.

Suzy's Story

Suzy at age eighty lives with her husband, a retired architect, in the same home in an established upscale neighborhood in a southern city where they raised their three children. She grew up and attended college and graduate school in the Northeast. Her interest was in science, and she wanted to attend medical school (even though almost no females were admitted at that time),[40] but her father felt that it was not an appropriate calling for a young lady. During World War II she worked in a microbiology lab and continued to work as a lab technician for a few years after she married and moved to Memphis. When she became a mother, she switched careers, took some education courses, and taught biology and chemistry in a private girls' high school.

Suzy and her husband have traveled extensively and led an active civic and social life, which has slowed down in recent years, as her husband's health is failing. She is still very active. She coordinates a church-sponsored tutoring program at a public grammar school where she also tutors twice a week. She plays tennis two or three times a week, keeps up with friends, drives carpools for her grandchildren, plays bridge, and regularly attends church and the theater.

A Word Portrait of Suzy

> Body?
> When you say body I think of the physical, the medical side
> of it—the parts, the workings, the functions, height, weight,
> coloring, health.
>
> Oh, the psychological is there. I think it fits.
> Attitude has a whole lot to do with how you feel.
> Some people are hypochondriacs and can find something
>   wrong with everything in their body,
> And everything outside their body.
>
> I am much more an optimist than a pessimist.
> I look on the positive side of things as much as I can.
> I can't speak for real maladies of the body—I enjoy good
>   health.
> I don't know what I would be if I were suddenly taken ill.
> I am blessed with good health.
> Real problems, real pain change people.
>
> Stay busy, stay real busy, do things, do a lot of things.
> You have to get outside yourself, reach out to other people.
> That takes your mind off your troubles,

You don't have time to think that maybe you have a pain
    somewhere or something.
I love to teach. The volunteer work I enjoy most is my
    tutoring—that is worthwhile.
I love to play—tennis two or three times a week and bridge,
A good game, a good social game.
It's fun.

As you grow older, you are not afraid of being.
You are not intimated by people as much.
You call a spade a spade.
My husband says I am opinionated.

I would have loved to have gone into medicine.
In those days it was almost impossible.
There was only one girl in a class of four hundred.
But my daughter is a doctor—that is a great pleasure for me.
I went on my own and got a master's degree. I worked during
    the war in labs.
I've taught science in high school.

I am a realist. Where I am in society is part of who I am.
When you get out in the world, you see what a small world
you live in
Intellectually, socially, and so forth.
There are other people who are very different.
There are a lot of people who are a whole lot smarter than I am.

There are a lot of people who are not—
They are much less fortunate in a lot of different ways.

I have a happy marriage, successful children (I've cried over
    them).
We have been very fortunate.
We have been blessed in so many ways—so happy.
This probably is part of my positive outlook.

Suzy's husband died several years after this interview, but her positive attitude and indomitable spirit continue to keep her connected

to life and other people of all ages. She calls herself a realist. She was trained and taught within the traditional biomedical paradigm, yet her attitude expands far beyond a purely physical, pathological definition of aging. The following chapters explore both cultural attitudes and recent scientific discoveries that support a rethinking of the orthodox view of aging, as well as some specific ways older people meet one of life's major transitions, the passage from middle to old age.

PART TWO

AGING THE NEW WAY

5

The Threshold

A cathedral may be made of bricks, but understanding the cathedralness of the structure is not limited to understanding bricks (nor even understanding the importance of buttresses that allow Gothic soaring). We may smash matter into particles, but understanding the material universe is not limited to understanding particles.

—*Karl H. Pribham, "Consciousness Reassessed"*

Most of us have heard the story of the Caribbean island Indians who marveled at the white men in strange costumes approaching their shore from out of the water. Where did these men come from? Surely they were gods appearing from the heavens. The Indians did not, could not, see Columbus's large ships with fluttering sails, anchored in the bay just fifty yards away. Such forms were beyond their experience, beyond their perception and comprehension, beyond their knowing. What those fifteenth-century Indians could see was limited by their *known* world. What we see in the twenty-first century is also limited by our *known* world.

In the 1840s a Hungarian doctor, Ignaz Semmelweis, practicing in a Vienna hospital, observed that impoverished peasant women under the care of hospital midwives were far less susceptible to childbirth fever than the wealthy women under the care of private physicians. Observing that physicians went straight from the morgue to the obstetric ward without washing their hands, Semmelweis wondered if there was a connection. After working on corpses, the doctors' hands were covered with blood and germs when they examined the new and expectant mothers. But at that time no one knew about germs. Blood on the hands and white coat of the doctor was a mark of prestige, indicating he was involved in serious research. Semmelweis devised his own experiment and began washing his hands before seeing his patients. Childbirth fever among those he saw disappeared. When he told his colleagues of his discovery and begged them to follow his example, they scoffed and laughed at such a preposterous procedure. It took forty years before Pasteur and Lister in the 1880s discerned the danger of germs. Their discoveries changed the *known* world of medical practitioners and prompted a new regime of cleanliness and antiseptics in hospital care.[1]

Today the incredible expansion of technology and vast dispersion of information seems to increase exponentially our known world daily. Our understanding of the way the known world operates is also changing. Science before the advent of quantum mechanics was predicated on the laws of Newtonian physics—cause and effect. If it cannot be measured, it does not exist. Observations of physical matter through microscopes led to knowledge of germs, bacteria, molecules, and genes. These discoveries were the grounding for great advances in the treatment of disease. A germ attacks a cell and creates a problem. A gene is inherited from a parent and causes a child's eyes to be brown. Biologists believed that if the stuff of life could be broken down to its most fundamental level, the mechanisms of the body would be understood, the causes of illness and aging predicted, and cures developed.

When another group of scientists, the nuclear physicists, started exploring the subatomic world, however, they could only observe and measure the tracings of minute entities rather than see a discernible object itself. They found that the component parts of atoms (the electrons, protons, and neutrons) did not conform to a Newtonian model of cause and effect. Although Newtonian laws are reliable in the gross world of buildings, bridges, aeronautical design, and orthodox medicine, in the subatomic realm of unbelievably tiny reality, the quantum physicists found that matter is in constant flux—sometimes behaving like a wave, sometimes like a particle. They found energy in motion, seemingly unpredictable and chaotic, continually moving, yet inherently interconnected. This startling revelation put a decidedly different perspective on reductive biomedical investigation. What if the body is not "inherently divisible"? What if the body and mind, in the final analysis, are not two different entities?

As quantum theory developed to explain these revolutionary findings, scientists came across another important revelation. Pure objectivity, in the traditional sense, the prerequisite of established scientific protocol, is impossible. The observer always influences the observation. The beliefs and assumptions held by scientists (or any observer) will influence the findings. One's point of view becomes part of the observation itself. Biologist Francisco Varela expressed it well when he said, "In my reality, knowledge coevolves with the knower and not as an outside, objective representation."[2] It is often very difficult, especially for classically trained scientists, to be aware that their assumptions affect the findings. Self-reflective analysis is not always a part of standard biomedical education.[3]

Evolving Knowledge

The two scientific disciplines, quantum physics and molecular biology, evolved independently until fairly recently, when a wealth of evidence began to demonstrate the importance of quantum theories for biological systems. New findings were bringing insights to biomedicine about the interconnectedness of the mind and body at a previously unimaginable level. Neurochemists, through research on the tiny particles of protein (the primary materials of life), created scientific evidence of a biochemical link between the body and mind. Through rigorous inquiry, Candace Pert, a creative iconoclast, demonstrated that emotional responses to lived experiences not only imprint on one's psyche, but they are transmitted at a molecular level throughout the substance of the body/mind systems. Pert found that neuropeptides, tiny particles of protein generated and distributed throughout the mind and body, are information carriers that operate independently of the central nervous system. This discovery upset the established notion of mind-body communication. For decades, most people thought that the brain and its extension, the central nervous system, was the primary electrical communication system within the body. It was "common" knowledge that the neurons, or nerve cells, which consist of a cell body with a tail-like axon and treelike dendrites, form something resembling a telephone system with trillions of miles of intricately criss-crossing wiring.[4]

This is in fact how the central nervous system operates, but Pert found that neuropeptides have their own highly complex network of communication that links all systems of the body (not just the nerves and brain) in an ongoing informational exchange. Pondering her discovery, she drew on quantum theory. "The mind as we experience it is immaterial, yet it has a physical substrate, which is *both* the body and the brain. It may also be said to have a nonmaterial, nonphysical substrate that has to do with the flow of . . . information."[5] Memories, both personal and collective, are stored throughout the body and provide the primary emotional and kinetic response to a situation. Your heartbeat quickens or your stomach grips when you are frightened. Your body is the seat of the unconscious that connects with what is happening below the thinking level. When you are frightened (or experience any type of emotional arousal), your body reacts first—oftentimes contrary to your rational intellect. Through discipline, practice, and experience, those initial body responses can be taught to respond in different ways, or at least be modified in their initial reactions. For example, many people dread public speaking. This fear can be overcome by speaking frequently and becoming comfortable in front of a crowd. This provides the body with new information based on learned experience. In familiar territory the body feels more at ease.

Before the discovery of the role of the chemical peptides in the body, it was generally believed that the three bodily systems—the *nervous* system (consisting of memory, thought, and emotion), the *immune* system (defending against invasive germs, repairing tissue, and healing wounds),[6] and the *endocrine* system (a glandular network controlling and regulating bodily functions)—each operated independently. Now we know they are inseparably linked. The three classically separated disciplines of neuroscience, endocrinology, and immunology (with their various organs—the brain; the glands; and the spleen, bone marrow, and lymph nodes) are actually joined to each other in a multidirectional network of communicating neuropeptides. And most importantly, human emotions trigger the production and activity of peptides that communicate with all systems simultaneously.

With inescapable evidence of the interconnectedness of all systems within the body and the brain, Pert courageously confronted the reductive, Cartesian/Newtonian framework of her biomedical profession as she demonstrated the major part emotions play in human health. "As I've watched as well as participated in this process [neurochemical research], I've come to believe that virtually all illness, if not psychosomatic in foundation, has a definite psychosomatic component."[7] At the molecular level, there is no distinction between the mind and the body—they are one.

Molecular chemist Bruce Lipton, who studies human cells in a petri dish, observes that beliefs influence body function and development at a cellular level. Lipton's observations of discrete cellular response in a controlled laboratory setting corroborate the importance of the body's emotional state on an individual's health. He found that at the most basic level, a dynamic force within each living cell adapts and reacts to the environment in which it is placed. Lipton's interpretation of this discovery seems to stand the reductive approach of classic molecular biology on its head. "It is the network of interactions in its entirety that constitutes and specifies the characteristics of a particular cell and not its components." Not only is the psychic aspect developed through interactions with one's environment and culture; the *soma*, too, is shaped by emotional encounters with both its internal and external environments.[8]

Biologists Humberto Maturana and Francisco Varela also emphasize the importance of context and environment on living matter when they take profound exception to the theory that genes alone contain the information that specify the characteristics and nature of a living being. "When we say that DNA contains what is necessary to specify a living being, we divest the components of their interrelation with the rest of the network."[9] Experiments on fully developed water fleas demonstrate that the genes of a living organism respond to their environment. Water fleas were placed in two separate tanks of water. The chemical scent of a predator fish was placed in one tank, and the fleas developed protective helmets that made them hard to swallow. The fleas in the other tank without the scent of danger did not grow helmets.[10] Part of the miracle and mystery of life is that cells or genes are not independent entities; at the most fundamental level, there is responsive exchange with their surroundings. However, the popular belief that one's genes determine one's body, one's health, the way one ages, is continually reinforced within our culture.

A 2005 newspaper article, headlined "Genes Tied to Exercise Benefits for Elderly," described research done at Wake Forest University involving 3,075 volunteers who were ages seventy through seventy-nine and healthy when the study began in 1997. The study lasted just over four years and found that those who exercised regularly were more likely to remain mobile than those who did not. The main focus of the article, however, was that those who enjoyed the greatest exercise benefit had inherited a particular gene.[11] According to the *Journal of American Medical Association* (*JAMA*), the geneticists had found a variation in the mobility among several genetic types, but their report said that "the physiological basis for these findings is uncertain. . . . Physically active participants (those reporting expending $\geq$ 1000 kcal/wk in exercise, walking, and stair climbing) were less likely to develop mobility limitation *regardless of genotype*" [emphasis added].[12] This, of course, is at variance with the results as reported in the popular media. The newspaper headline and article inferred that genes made the difference in the mobility of the elderly, whereas the original research reported in *JAMA* stated that exercise, not genotype, was the determining factor in mobility. Such reporting tends to reinforce a mind-set that places reliance on scientific expertise and undermines the individual elder's responsibility for maintaining his or her own mobility.

The important news is that if an aging person exercises, he or she will retain mobility regardless of gene type. The continual reinforcement of the belief in genetic determinism is discouraging and misleading. Media news, filled with scientific findings from reductive molecular biology and pharmaceutical claims, perpetuates the simplification. According to cell biologist Richard C. Strohman, "Medical research continues to be dominated by molecular/genetic analysis and by a reductionist program that resists any tendency towards analysis in which the gene appears not as sole causal agent but merely as an important part of the overall complex biological system."[13]

Lamenting that biomedical research rarely addresses issues of wellness, Strohman adds that most government and private funding research budgets are assigned to genetic-related problems. "The problem here is that, while the HGP [Human Genome Project] (research completed in 2003 that identified the approximately 20,000–25,000 genes in human DNA and determined the chemical sequences of their components) will be able to provide a detailed genetic map for complex polygenic diseases, it cannot provide the instructions for reading these maps." He says the HGP will provide few insights into the vast majority of complex human diseases or aid in their prevention because the secrets of health and wellness are not reducible solely to the actions of single or even multiple genetic agents. "There is no theoretical insight into the concepts of wellness and health from fundamental research in experimental biology centered in a reductionistic genetics. Concepts of health and wellness are characteristics of whole organisms and of processes that are time and place dependent—dynamic processes open to environmental signals and contextualized by an individual's life experience."[14] The conventional approach, which focuses on finding the tiny bits of matter that make you sick—germs, virus, parasites, or aberrant specks of DNA—has been highly successful in thwarting infectious disease but does little to nothing to promote healing. We now need to focus on what makes us well, and many people are seeking new answers.

Although governmental funding, pharmaceutical research, advertising, and the media consider (either consciously or unconsciously) the body from a conventional perspective, within recent decades alternatives to allopathic medicine are attracting more and more attention. In 1998 almost half of adult Americans visited a practitioner of alternative medicine, exceeding the total number of visits that year to mainstream physicians, such as family physicians, internists, pediatricians, and gynecologists.[15] Since that time, the public's preference for alternative and complementary medicine continues to grow stronger, and some biomedical researchers, educators, and practitioners are beginning to accept and respect the mind-body connection. The deep-seated bias favoring orthodoxy prevails in most medical schools, however, perpetuating the reductive allopathic construct among most medical practitioners.[16] But there have been exceptions among the classically trained physicians.

Christiane Northrup, M.D. (ob-gyn), is such an exception. A courageous medical pioneer, Northrup left an established group practice of obstetrics and gynecology in 1985 and established Women to Women to provide educational and medical services to women from women in Yarmouth, Maine. She, with another female ob-gyn and two nurse practitioners, founded a clinic to bring holistic understanding and treatment into the context of conventional medical care. Northrup herself had confronted a serious medical problem a few years before when her own babies were born. Battling to meet demanding job requirements, while nursing her first-born, she developed a serious breast infection, which she ignored. Her training had conditioned her to put her own needs last—she did not want to be labeled "weak or incapable of pulling her own weight" by her male colleagues. Finally, she became so ill she had to quit work and undergo surgery. After problems with nursing her second child (she believed mother's milk was essential for the baby's well-being) and seemingly insurmountable demands in every phase of her life, she, as she put it, "came unglued." Her whole understanding of her life as a doctor, wife, and mother underwent radical adjustment. She believes her body was sending a powerful message. Northrup became profoundly aware of the impact of emotions on health. Her formal medical training and working culture (almost all male at that time) had put her in deep denial of the realization that "a woman's health is completely tied up with the culture in which she lives and her position within it, as well as in the way she lives her life as an individual."[17] Realizing that she had a choice to forge a new model for working mothers, she established her clinic. Her commitment was to look at all aspects of a woman's life in order to activate healing. "Improving habits and diet alone is not enough to effect a permanent cure for conditions that have been present for a long time. . . . true healing will never occur until a woman learns to trust the wisdom of her body."

Because Northrup's writing, teaching, and practice were directly contrary to the prevailing views of her profession at that time, she feared censure from her colleagues. This stress created tremendous personal anxiety; she fundamentally respected the benefits of traditional medical treatments and the skills of her colleagues. She felt it extremely important to maintain her professional relationships. Over time, the tension eased and she gained the validation of her peers as the women she taught and treated responded to her message. "Our bodies are influenced and actually structured by our beliefs. . . . *Hope, self-esteem, and education are the most important factors in creating health daily,* no matter what our background or the state of our health in the past.[18]

The philosophy underlying Northrup's book *Women's Bodies, Women's Wisdom,* though written for women, serves as a model for confronting the cultural myths about aging bodies, be they male or female. Below is an adaptation of a chart from her book that offers an elegant view of our bodies as process, regardless of our age.

The Body as a Process vs. Medical Worldview[19]

The Body as a Process	Medical Worldview
The body reflects nature and earth	The body and its processes are uncontrollable and unreliable. They require external control.
Thoughts and emotions are mediated via the immune, endocrine, and nervous systems.	Thoughts and emotions are entirely separate from the physical body. They are biochemical events.
The physical, emotional, spiritual, and psychological aspects of an individual are intimately intertwined and cannot be separated.	It is possible to separate an individual into entirely separate, unrelated compartments.
Illness is part of the inner guidance system.	Illness is a random event that just happens. There is very little a person can do to prevent illness.
The body creates health daily. It is inherently self-healing.	The body is always vulnerable to germs, disease, and decay.
Illness is best prevented by living fully according to one's inner guidance while creating health daily.	Illness prevention is not possible in this system. So-called prevention is really disease screening.
Concern is with living fully. Focus on what is going well without denying death.	Concern is with avoiding death at all costs. Focus on what can go wrong.
Life is perpetual.	Death is seen as failure and final.

The Placebo Effect

There are still many unanswered questions. Some may never be explained, but a holistic understanding of the mind/body/spirit provides clues. The placebo effect is a case in point. The word *placebo,* when first used in the Middle Ages, meant "I shall please." It referred to professional mourners who were hired to accompany funeral processions to the graves. Since this beginning the word has carried a somewhat pejorative spin, implying deception or quackery. In modern times, as the term was adopted in the medical arena, *placebo* referred to a "dummy pill" or benign deception. Physicians usually made a negative assessment of patients who responded to placebos. Attending doctors felt that nothing was really wrong. Their patients were not really sick, just malingering—faking it. The problem was all in the mind (which, of course, was completely separate from the body). Over the last couple of decades this attitude has changed, however. Medical researchers are giving placebos a second look in an effort to understand double-blind trials and experiments that demonstrate that the placebo is as effective, or sometimes even more effective, than drug-based medication or invasive corrective surgery.

In 1994 J. Bruce Moseley, the team physician for the Houston Rockets and a surgeon at the Houston Veterans Affairs Medical Center, participated in an elaborate form of "make-believe" to test the efficacy of arthroscopic surgery for arthritis of the knee. At the time Moseley gave little heed to mind/body theories but was growing skeptical of the benefits of arthroscopic surgery. After agreeing to participate in a very unorthodox experiment, he helped convince the institutional review board to sanction it. Ten middle-aged men suffering from knee pain volunteered to take part in this peculiar study. They were informed that all would be prepped, draped, and wheeled into the operation room for sedation. However, only two of the ten would receive general anesthesia and undergo standard arthroscopic procedure—scraping and rinsing of the knee joint. Three of the men would have rinsing alone. Five would be given a light sedation, and Moseley would stab their knees a couple of times with a scalpel so they would have an incision and scars after the procedure. Postoperatively all of the men were to be dispatched to the recovery room and sent home the next morning with crutches and pain medication. So Dr. Moseley would not unconsciously "give away the secret," he did not know whom he would operate on and who would receive the placebo treatment until he was in the operating room and the patient sedated. Six months after the surgery, none of the ten patients knew which procedure he had received. But all ten reported much less pain, and none was unhappy with the results.[20] For those ten men, placebo surgery was successful. The importance, or necessity, of professional ministration for the success is still an unanswered question.

Irving Kirsch, a psychologist at the University of Connecticut, and Guy Sapirstein of the Westwood Lodge Hospital in Needham, Massachusetts, published results of their clinical trials of antidepressants. They concluded that the expectation of improvement, not adjustments, in brain chemistry, accounted for 75 percent of the drugs' effectiveness. Kirsch emphasizes that it is our beliefs, not drugs, that constitute the critical factor in transformation. Speculation on the reasons for effectiveness will continue. They all point to holistic understanding.[21]

Michael Loes, M.D., the director of the Arizona Pain Institute, an education and research program associated with the University of Arizona's Integrative Program in Anesthesiology, believes that belief creates biology. Humans think with their cells, not with their brains. He feels that understanding body intelligence and nature's efforts to preserve homeostasis are the keys to understanding pain. A cardinal factor for health is the individual's perception of pain. Using arthritis as an example, Loes illustrates that pain accompanying acute inflammation is a component of the natural healing process. However, the patient's attempts to ignore or mask this acute pain, rather than changing lifestyle and possibly attitude and self-perceptions, can lead to chronic inflammation and a smoldering, self-perpetuating cellular response. This then leads to further complications, stagnation, and greater loss of function.[22]

A New Era in Medicine

Larry Dossey, M.D., a strong advocate for the power of nonlocal (spiritual) medicine, is forging a radically new epistemology for the contemporary medical arena. To give historical perspective to the development of modern medicine, Dossey divides its evolution into three eras:[23]

- ERA I—*Mechanical, material, or physical medicine.* A Newtonian view of reality governs, in which classical laws of cause and effect rule matter and energy. Physical reality is determined by causative principles. Mind is not a factor in illness. Mind is the result of brain mechanisms. Therapy focuses solely on the effects of *things* in the body with a reliance on drugs, surgery, irradiation, CPR, and so forth, and more recently gene therapy. With confidence in high-tech solutions, the basic assumption is that every disease, once diagnosed should be treatable.

• ERA II—*Mind/body medicine.* An appreciation of the power of the mind in "psychosomatic" disease and that the mind is a major factor in healing *within* the single person. The mind has causal power. Medicine is not fully explainable by classic concepts of physics. Era II includes, but goes beyond, Era I with an emphasis on therapy such as psychoneuroimmunology, counseling, hypnosis, biofeedback, relaxation, and imagery-based therapies. The effects of consciousness are believed to reside *solely* within the individual body.

• ERA III—*Nonlocal, eternity medicine.* Mind is a factor in healing both *within* and *between* persons. Mind is not completely localized to points in space (brains or bodies) or time (present moment or single lifetimes). Mind is unbounded in space and time and thus is ultimately unitary or one. Era III incorporates a holistic view of mind/body/spirit. New knowledge in a subsequent era does not mean that all former theories and practices should be discarded. It means that old theories must be considered in light of new (sometimes ancient) and expanded discoveries and practice. It is not an either/or situation.

Dossey feels that each era built on the previous one; the discoveries and practices of Era I were the foundation of that which was developed in Era II, and the two previous eras are invaluable to Era III. While acknowledging all this, however, he emphasizes that it is essential that the contributions of each previous era must be rethought in light of new understandings and the limitations or errors of that era recognized.[24]

A New View of Old Age

Dossey's analysis of the three eras of modern medicine provides a natural bridge for recasting our understanding of old age. Since the beginning of the twentieth century, old age in the United States has been defined as a pathology to be cured by biomedical experts. In that context the body was viewed as a complex mechanism apart from the mind. New understanding of aging is needed as we enter the twenty-first century. Aging and old age must be understood in their total context. This in no way negates the value of biomedical accomplishments. They are legion, but old age is not an infection or acute illness or even a deviant gene.

Again drawing from the insights of Richard C. Strohman, who takes issue with the allopathic approach to aging, "There is overwhelming evidence that increases in life expectancy have come in the past [to older people] through holistic measures and not from applications of medical technology. At the same time, the community of fundamental biological researchers, as exemplified by current directions within the National Institutes of Health and the Human Genome Project, continue to emphasize a molecular/ genetic approach." Explaining that theoretically this approach could marginally extend the lives of the affluent few for a couple of years, he argues that it would be far wiser to balance research focus on the more complex issues of living organisms and their interactions with the world in which they live.[25]

We have entered a new era of understanding of what it means to be old in the United States. Our known world has shifted. Definitive research demonstrates the importance of attitude and behavior on aging. There is growing recognition that body/mind/spirit are inseparably linked within the human organism. This holistic understanding has far-reaching implications not only for the aging individual but also for the care and treatment of the elderly. It does not mean we need to choose between biomedical knowledge and holistic knowledge. The choice is not *either/or* but *both/and.* It is not choosing one worldview over another but appreciating the values in both. Integrative medicine is becoming an exciting reality.

In 2003 the first $100,000 Bravewell Leadership Award for Integrative Medicine was presented to Ralph Snyderman, M.D., Chancellor for Health Affairs of Duke University Health System. Dr. Snyderman's commitment is to blending the best in scientific and technological medical approaches with a humanist, holistic understanding of people's needs, and openness to the fact that science and technology cannot address all our health problems. Another one of the finalists, Brian Berman, M.D., of the University of Maryland Medical School, commented, "Just over ten years ago, not long after I started the integrative medicine center, I met a friend's father, then the dean of one of New York's medical schools. When he heard what I was trying to do, he spoke with the directness he is respected for: It was 'a load of hogwash.' I was greatly surprised, therefore, to hear an address he gave recently, entitled 'Complementary and Integrative Medicine.' In his straightforward manner, he was calling on his colleagues to take an active role and see what this had to offer to improve medicine. We have come a long way."[26]

Professional caregivers, medical practitioners, and social workers are being offered new insights and information. When treating the elderly, will they see beyond diseased tissue, frail forms, or statistical norms? Will they recognize the holistic reality of the living, feeling, responsive individual? Aging is a natural process not to be conquered or denied but understood, so that humans can creatively live this phase of life to the fullest, rather than be defined by limiting cultural stereotypes. When will mainstream medicine, the media, and our culture get the message?

The words of the late psychoanalyst Erik Erikson ring true. "Lacking a culturally viable ideal of old age, our civilization does not really harbor a concept of the whole of life."[27] New assumptions about aging must be learned by people of *all* ages. The challenge for older people is to recognize destructive cultural patterns that shape our view of aging and consciously make new choices that bring coherence to our lives as we grow old.

In rethinking our cultural assumptions, we should bear in mind the words of C. G. Jung: "To the constantly reiterated question "What can I do?" I know no other answer except, become what you have always been, namely the wholeness which we have lost in the midst of our civilized, conscious existence, a wholeness which we always were without knowing it."[28] Jung believed that the second half of life should be devoted to individuation. Individuation is a personal task to uncover the self that lies beneath and beyond the personal ego that has been formed through adaptation to culture. Individuation is conscious living in appreciation and a sense of wonder for the wholeness of body/mind/spirit. It calls one to be consciously in harmony with the rhythms and cycles of nature. Aging is not a battle to be won; aging is part of our natural life to be intentionally lived. It may bring us to a new appreciation of where we are in the cosmos, as reflected in my recent meditation on the fifteenth anniversary of my mother-in-law, Memo's death, (Memo was the name our children called her).

On the One Hundred and Fourth Anniversary of Memo's Birth

An evening, after supper stroll down to lakeside
Brought ethereal repose.
Soft, yet brilliant, diffused light of dusk,
A gentle, bare wisp of breeze,
Stillness disrupted only by an occasional flutter of a swooping gull.
No evidence of other humans,
Save for the distant light three miles across the water.
I stand soaking in serenity.
Blessed.
The pines behind stand
A part of the moment,
A part of me.
The water laps.
My beagle pups sniff, crunch pebbles,
We are one
In the ethereal.
Within, without, unending.

6

Insights for Aging

> There is something you can tell people over and over, and with feeling and eloquence, and still never say it well enough for it to be more than news from abroad—people have no readiness for it, no empathy. It is the news of personal aging—of climbing, and knowing it, to some unrepeatable pitch and coming forth on the other side, which is pleasant still but which is, unarguably, different—which is the beginning of descent.
>
> —*Mary Oliver,* Winter Hours

I have passed the midpoint of my life. In fact, I am well into the descent. But contrary to the popular connotation of equating descent with decline, I view this descent as a call to explore myself more fully, to descend into the depths of being, and to probe this experience of aging as a new and extraordinary phase of human living. I am fortunate. When I began to experience the very disorienting feeling of stepping into a new phase of life, I found the works of Carl Jung and various other philosophies and psychologies that helped me to understand the interworkings of the human mind and spirit. Through readings, conversations, counseling, and study I found a map for my descent. This was not a simple road map with explicit directions, a how-to, ten-step formula for growing old. The map I discovered was more like a vast topographical display of gigantic mountains, hidden valleys, mysterious caves, expansive valleys, treacherous ravines, quiet forest glens, threatening whirlpools, and hot, dry deserts. It was a multifaceted vision of the human spirit and psyche created from the vantage point of Jung's years of observation, counseling, and living within the Western milieu, as well as his extended exploration and study of cultures other than early twentieth-century European. And most important were his profound reflections on his own thoughts and feelings from his long and vast professional and personal experience. Jung's reflections, insights from his followers, and wisdom from other traditions gave me a sense of direction for my journey of a descent into self.

Gifts from Carl Jung

Jung grew up in the Protestant Victorian culture of late nineteenth-century Switzerland, a culture that greatly influenced the values of America during that period. His father was a pastor. On completion of medical school in the early 1900s, Jung became a psychiatrist and disciple of Sigmund Freud, the brilliant doctor from Vienna who was the acknowledged leader in the emerging "science" of psychiatry. Freud was breaking new ground with his revolutionary ideas and iconoclastic theories about the power of the unconscious mind. Freud believed the roots of human behavior are hidden mental processes or complexes that are not accessible to the conscious mind and can only be revealed through in-depth psychoanalysis, a protocol that he developed. According to Freud, each individual person is an independent bundle of psychic complexes molded through familial relationships in infancy. He believed that the single most important factor for explaining adult behavior is childhood experiences that are recorded in the unconscious and irretrievable except through depth analysis. Freudian theory, based on the scientific determinism of the time, gives primacy to the sexual drive as the life force (the *libido*) that shapes the development of the ego and behavior of an adult.

The exclusivity of the sexual drive in defining the adult libido is the central point that precipitated an early break for Jung with his mentor, although he completely agreed with Freud on the power of the unconscious in shaping human behavior. For these two intellectual giants the human psyche could be compared to a giant iceberg—the conscious mind is like the small exposed tip that is seen above the waterline; the far greater part, the unconscious mind, lies unseen, hidden beneath the surface. According to Jung, the unconscious contains complexes (archetypes) that are universal to all human experience. These archetypes comprise the collective unconscious that lies beneath an individual's personal unconscious connecting all of humanity at a fundamental level and are a part of everyone's psyche. The collective unconscious, a repository of human experience beyond the personal psyche is difficult to apprehend but is revealed in the myths, legends, and spiritual traditions of people the world over. Jung believed that part of the energy force in everyone's personal libido was a deep and ever-present (though not always conscious) need to connect with the ineffable, spiritual realm that lies beyond self, buried in the collective unconscious. The drive of an individual to connect with the numinous, mysterious forces of reality found in the collective unconscious is an essential element of human development.

Jung and Freud had vastly different views on aging. Freudian theory suggests that there is not much point in older people getting in touch with their unconscious because they do not have enough libido in them for a change to occur. He wrote that "near or about the age of fifty the elasticity of the mental processes . . . is, as a rule, lacking—old people are no longer educable."[1] Jung, on the other hand, believed that one's midforties are the midpoint of life, which calls for a radical transition in one's psychological focus to continue learning as one enters a new phase.

In Jung's understanding, a newborn lives in the unconscious. There is no discrimination between the conscious and unconscious psyche at birth. A child begins to develop an ego in response to outside forces in his or her early years. The psychological task during the first half of life is conquering, accommodating, and adjusting to the external. Developing an ego is very necessary for an individual to live successfully in society. But on reaching midlife, in order to continue to progress psychologically, Jung believed we must turn inward. He believed that this *metanoia*, or turning back to the unconscious, is the primary task of the second half of life. If life's energy (libido) is directed outward toward the outer world in the first half of life, and then inward toward the inner world during the second half of life, it remains active, alive, and vivifying; the human being remains both physically and psychologically energized. Jung goes on to say that if a person does not make the shift inward during the second half of life, the libido is then the catalyst for deterioration and decay.[2]

Jung believed that an active, productive life prepares a person for the necessary transition. An adult's first task is to focus emotional and intellectual energies outward and learn to harness one's libido to develop a strong ego, get along with others, achieve personal goals, and master skills for producing a livelihood. Adults are not ready until midlife (after learning to cope and adjust to external forces) to go within to explore their inner selves. The exploration of the psyche requires a totally new focus in a different direction. The beginning point is a well-formed ego. Older people who continue to judge themselves on previously valued criteria will likely become discouraged when they find they do not have as much effect on the outside world. This easily leads to an attitude that "it does not matter what I do," and is a prime cause of depression among the old. When an older individual finds his or her personal worth only through approval or accolades from others, disappointment (that can lead to depression) is almost inevitable.

Aging is an individual journey. Individuals respond to their environment and process information very differently.[3] It is not always easy. One starts the journey into self-discovery beyond culture to forge awareness and build new understanding of the unconscious forces that shape what it means to be human both personally and collectively. The inward journey not only makes one face his or her personal demons, but it ultimately leads to deeper connections with the spiritual dimension of life itself, which Jung "knew" lay at the heart of reality. He is often quoted for saying, "I do not believe in God; I know God."

Jung's knowledge of God was universal, far beyond the limitation of time and culture. He found the same truths at the heart of all of the world's religions and saw religious institutions and theologies as cultural constructions that too often preclude individuals from touching the mysterious reality of the divine. He had tremendous respect and awe for the power of personal growth throughout the whole of life. The urge of the individual's quest at midlife into her or his own psyche is a creative journey away from the strictures of inherited and embedded institutional beliefs that are built through accommodations to the outside world.

As individuals delve into their inner selves, they become increasingly aware of life in its totality. The timing and sequence of individual journeys differ, but every well-adjusted elder faces each task at various times along the way. Jungians Bruce Baker and Jane Wheelwright identified seven steps (or psychological-spiritual tasks) for the journey into old age.[4]

- The first step is normally in the late fifties or early sixties when *the reality of death is accepted.* Younger people almost always associate any age over sixty with death. However, most older folks seldom think about it. They focus on living and accept death as part of life. Older people know death is there but consider it as Goethe did, *nature's expert advice to get plenty of life*. The old person who is greedy, childish, churlish, defiant, and/or fearful is often the person who cannot face death—the healthy psyche at the end of life accepts death as a part of life.

- The second important task for old age is a reflection and *review of the sum of one's life*. There is value in frequent reminiscing and the collection of the various strands of one's life from earlier years. This act of witnessing one's own life helps individuals see their lives for what they are and helps prepare them for the next step.

- The third step—*accepting the reality that our lives have finite limits*. Though many of these limits are recognized and accepted along the way, they need to be consciously acknowledged. Time in its relentless advance makes certain experiences unattainable. Some careers will never be followed, some children will never be born, one may never climb Mt. Everest or write the great American novel, some relationships will never be resolved, desired achievements in one's chosen field may become improbable, if not impossible. Conscious mental boundaries need to be drawn and what were once thought to be cherished goals reassessed and perhaps abandoned. The conscious letting go of these burdens and aspirations formed in earlier years lets one focus total attention and energy not only on what is attainable, but also on what is one's truest concern. It is a time when new and possibly very different goals are established.

- The fourth task, *letting go of the dominance of the ego*, is extremely difficult unless the first three steps have been taken. Jung spoke of the letting-go process, which occurs after one learns to touch and begin to assimilate the unconscious. Letting go creates "an approximation of conscious and unconscious where the center of the personality no longer coincides with the ego, but with a point midway between the conscious and the unconscious."[5] Letting go of the ego is very difficult, especially for those who have been highly successful and productive in business or a profession, or found life's meaning through shepherding their own growing children. The more rewards and esteem a person has received from society for outstanding productivity and success, the less likely it will be that he or she can let go of ego dominance without a struggle. The focus outward is deeply ingrained in the psyche of such a person. Letting go of dependable self-concepts and habits of the heart is truly a challenge. To the highly productive individual, the process of looking inward seems self-indulgent, weak, and nonproductive. Going within to confront the shadow side of one's inner reality can be very painful,[6] even though it is necessary for achieving integration of the total self.

• The fifth task of aging is *encountering and honoring the true Self.* Jungians distinguish the true Self from the ego-driven "false self" that is oriented to the outside world. The false self (the Jungian term is *persona*) is characterized by fear and thrives on judgment, cynicism, anger, blame, and shame. Such negative attitudes reinforce the illusion that we are separate from other people and from the natural world and tend to increase anxiety and negative patterns of thought. The true Self is realized when the conscious personality connects with the all-inclusive voice from the depths of one's being. The thoughts of the true Self center on creativity, inspiration, sharing, caring, forgiveness, gratitude, love, and the actualization of potential.[7] Jung saw the true Self as "God within."[8]

• The sixth step is recognizing and acknowledging that the *Self is God within.* When we consciously build bridges that create links to the unconscious and God, we will come to a richer and fuller understanding of the meaning of our lives in old age.

• The seventh step, the most far-reaching and most often uncompleted aspect of aging, is *the engagement of unused potentials.* One experiences the unleashing and encouragement of one's creativity that may have been stifled or restricted since childhood by a strong ego and a need to conform to outside pressures or, in many cases, lack of time. Children naturally create through play. Stepping into old age provides an opportunity to tap into that long-buried potential for creativity and learn again the delights of play. Living itself becomes the point. The unexpected becomes the raw material for exploring life. A radically new approach is needed for the fulfillment of this step in the journey into old age, but the rewards are great. To describe the life of the wise elder, I have paraphrased something that Jung once wrote about the life of the artist. The wise elder is not a person endowed with free will who seeks her or his own end, but an individual who allows age to realize its purposes through the true Self. As a human being he or she may have moods and wills and personal aims, but the wise elder is human in a higher sense—he or she is "collective elder," a vehicle and molder of the unconscious psychic life of humankind.[9]

Jung's great prescription for creative living into old age is the realization that we belong to something far greater than self and culture. Only through conscious awareness, the expansion of a narrow, culturally framed view of reality, can we hope to tap into the underlying font of creativity. Although the unconscious, both personal and collective, will never be fully known, there are symbols of discernible archetypal patterns revealed in dreams, myths, traditions, and the arcane arts. These symbols are metaphors for interpreting numinous truths normally obscured to conscious reality. Taken literally or at face value, the meaning within such metaphors is seldom revealed. We must learn to trust the nonrational, the imagination, as an equal partner with the rational in exploring the deeper meanings within what Jung termed these "messages from God." His passion was to bring contemporary appreciation of the collective unconscious and help individuals connect with it in meaningful ways. These were not new ideas. Much of his understanding was drawn from the wisdom of the ancients.

Demeter and Persephone

On the north coast of continental Africa, now Libya, lie the ruins of the ancient Greek city of Cyrene. Founded around 630 B.C.E., in the classical world, Cyrene was a center of agriculture, commerce, and culture for a millennium. An earthquake in 262 C.E. and ensuing climatic changes after that time caused a slow decline of this once-thriving metropolis. Today, because its ruins were not ravaged by marauding armies or covered over by layers of subsequent civilizations, as is true of many ancient cities, Cyrene is a relatively pure archaeological treasure.[10] On the outskirts of Cyrene the terraces of a sanctuary of Demeter, the Goddess of the Harvest, offer an invitation to step into the sacred place of the honored tradition and faith that sustained the people of that time. Demeter and her daughter Persephone were some of the most revered goddesses of ancient times; the symbolism within their story carries profound relevance for us today.

Metaphorical symbols within such ancient myths are archetypal. They relate to the universality of all human experience, both male and female. "Masculine" and "feminine" in myth interpretation are symbolic expressions used to denote the opposing psychic impulses within all individuals, regardless of sex, and do not refer to physical or sexual characteristics. The symbolism of male and female entities within myths is similar to the use of yin and yang in Eastern philosophies. Truths found in goddess legends do represent female experience at one level, but at a deeper level they represent the psychic/spiritual experience of both male and female. In the collective unconscious, at the deepest level, the true Self, is an androgynous composite. Within the psyche of every man resides the multitude of feminine complexes, just as a woman's psyche contains at some level all archetypal male impulses. To explore the symbolic meaning of a myth, we must identify with every character in the story, just as in dream analysis we must realize that we are every part of our dream—the good, the bad, the powerful, and the passive. Both myths and dreams give us powerful images.

The psyche's language is that of image and not idea. Christine Downing implores us to live the myths by absorbing the images into our own lives. The psyche needs images to nurture its own growth, for images provide a knowledge that we interiorize rather than apply.[11] It is often difficult to know how an archetypal image bears on our own life, but when we suspend judgment and identify with the symbol (walk in the symbol's shoes, so to speak), understanding of what lies deeply buried in the unconscious percolates and broadens our perspective. When I read the myth of Demeter and Persephone, I am Demeter; I am Persephone. I am Hecate. I am Zeus and Hades and also contain the potential of Hermes, the messenger. Different truths about my own life emerge each time I return to the story. Of course, each time I am at a different place in my life.

There are many versions of Demeter's story and an equal number of interpretations. That is the power of myth—they speak to us in many ways at various levels. Here is the story as told in the Hymn to Demeter.[12]

Demeter, the fair-haired earth goddess who blesses all phases of harvest, was known to display her moods by producing both feast and famine. Zeus, the ruler of the Olympian gods, was the father of Demeter's daughter Persephone. The hymn tells of Persephone, as a lovely young maiden, at play picking flowers. These were not earthly flowers, however. They were the work of Zeus, put there for "a girl with a flower's beauty." These flowers were a beautiful, divine trap for Persephone. The trigger for the trap was an irresistible flower with one hundred stems of fragrant blossoms. When Persephone reached out with both hands to pluck this flower, the earth opened at her feet. Hades, king of the underworld, roared forth in his golden chariot and seized her before an alarm could be sounded. No mortal on the earth heard Persephone's pleas for help before she vanished into the Underworld. Of the immortals, only two heard the faint cries of the abducted girl—Hecate, goddess of darkness, and Helios, god of the sun.

When Persephone disappeared, her mother, Demeter, searched in vain for her daughter. The mother's sorrow was so great that she denied herself all food, drink, and comfort for nine days. When dawn arrived on the tenth day, Hecate came to Demeter and told her that she had heard a voice but had not seen the abduction of poor Persephone. The two goddesses went to Helios because he sees all mortal and immortal actions. Helios, indeed, knew the plot and the players. He told Demeter that Zeus and Hades were responsible for Persephone's entrapment. He further advised her to accept the situation because Hades was lord of many and not an unseemly bridegroom. Demeter did not like his advice and chose a long, brooding path to regain her precious daughter. Disguising herself as a mature mortal woman, she became the servant of a noble couple and nanny for their infant son. Demeter worked to steal the boy's loyalty and affection away from his parents (just as her daughter had been stolen from her). She tried to transform the young boy into an immortal by placing him in the fireplace, but before Demeter (still in disguise) could make the boy immortal, this boy's mother recognized the goddess for who she was and stopped the ceremony. With her failure to gain a new child, Demeter's wrath took a deadlier turn. The following year, no seed sprouted. No barley grew in the plowed fields. All mortals were doomed to famine and eventual destruction if Demeter did not lift her curse. Zeus tried to dissuade Demeter from her ruinous course, but the goddess of harvest was unmoved. Then all the immortals came to her, begging her to change her mind and give life back to the earth. She refused them all. Finally, Zeus sent Hermes to the underworld to speak with Hades and Persephone. Hermes explained the situation and suggested, with gentle words, that Persephone be returned to her mother. Hades was filled with compassion, but he was also intent on keeping his bride. He gave Persephone a honey-sweet pomegranate seed as she departed. By tasting the seed, she became eternally bound to Hades and the underworld.

Demeter was overjoyed when she saw her darling Persephone again, but her joy was tempered by the fact that Hades had tricked the innocent Persephone (feeding her the pomegranates) so that she must eventually return to him. In an effort to save the earth and appease Demeter, Zeus promised that Persephone could spend two-thirds of the year with her mother, but the remaining third of the year would be spent with her husband, Hades, in the underworld. Demeter agreed, and the earth began to swiftly recover its vitality and became fertile again.

What do all these symbols mean to us in today's world, so vastly different from that of mythical Demeter? In Demeter we see the great mother, Mother Earth, font of all life, tested and ultimately accepting the cyclical nature of all creation. Some interpretations of the legend focus on the rape of the maiden and the manipulative power of male energy within a patriarchal culture; others see a father honoring and promoting the maturing of a daughter by fostering her step into womanhood. There is also the fury of a mother on losing her child—Demeter's consummate rage as she wrecks havoc on all within her power and her duplicity in trying to replace lost affection by stealing another's child. If the underworld is symbolic of the unconscious, we see Persephone, queen of the underworld, awakened to her own sense of self as she tastes the fruits of primal energy, although she subsequently chooses to return to the light of the conscious world and reunite with her mother (or the "mothering" part of herself) and live in the light of conscious reality. Hades, king of the underworld, is depicted as possessive, yet compassionate. When the myth is taken as metaphor for multiple complexes within individual and collective psychics, the extraordinary complexity of feelings, roles, and impulses present in the ongoing, natural cycle of self renewal is revealed.

Other ancient cultures have stories similar to the legend of Demeter and Persephone. The goddesses Ishtar of Akkadia, Inanna of the

Sumerians, and the Semitic Astarte, as well as the Egyptian God Osiris, each in his or her own culture ruled fertility, lived part of the year in the underworld, and were transformed anew every spring in accord with nature's cycle. Peter Kingsley, scholar of pre-Socratic Greece, in his book *In the Dark Places of Wisdom* (a title that captures a profound concept) writes about the centrality of the Demeter/Persephone myth to ancient Greece and the rituals and personal practices of the people.[13] A prevalent practice of the ancients was the "incubation of the soul." In the belief that access to the unconscious was necessary for health and healing (and what moderns might call personal growth), three or four days were spent periodically alone in caves in a state of absolute stillness and dream interpretation. Today's culture creates few opportunities for the incubation of the soul.

Another insight we garner from Greek mythology is from Apollo—the god of truth, the god of light, the god of healing. According to an Orphic poem Apollo (the healer) and Persephone (the goddess of the unconscious and the realm of the dead) made love. Here we find a metaphor for the intimate connection between the power of healing, the unconscious, and death. The ancients believed that ultimately there is no real healing (of body and soul) without the ability to face death itself. To heal is to know the limits of healing and also what lies beyond. The ancients give us profound insights into the whole of life.

Connecting with the Unconscious

Symbols representing the hidden numinous reality in which we live are found throughout the history of all cultures and religions. But, all too often, the rich symbolism within the traditions of today's established religions have been lost to contemporary worshipers who are grounded in the concept that all reality is material. Jungians and other spiritual leaders search beyond material authentication to see that dreams, myths, legends, and the arcane arts[14] are fruitful avenues for exploring the deeper meaning of human experience. Rather than eschew the occult, astrology, and Tarot as arcane artifacts with little meaning for the modern scientific world, Jung found these traditions rich in symbolism for accessing the concepts and complexes that reside within the great unconscious.

The unconscious and the conscious exist in a profound state of interdependence of each other and the well-being of one is impossible without the well-being of the other. If ever the connection between these two great states of being is diminished or impaired, man becomes sick and deprived of meaning; if the flow between one and the other is interrupted for long, the human spirit and life on earth are re-plunged in chaos and old night [depression].[15]

Intuition is needed along with intellect. The health of the whole person depends on what Jung called awareness, the building of nonrational (we might say illogical) bridges between the conscious and the ever-expanding, ultimately incomprehensible universe of the unconscious. For some the spreading of Tarot cards creates one of these nonrational bridges. Tarot cards, which have existed in one form or another for at least six centuries, contain rich symbolism of ancient wisdom and mystical lore from such fields as alchemy, Gnosticism, and astrology. For Jungians, the spreading of the cards is not a means to predict the future, but a means to create one of those nonrational bridges into the unconscious. The rich symbolism of Tarot cards tells the eternal story of everyman's and everywoman's journey through life as one of unending and recurring cyclical progression. The spreading of the Tarot is an opportunity to contemplate the profound patterns within the depths of human experience and consider the relationship of underlying archetypes (psychic patterns) to one's current situation. Joseph Campbell's book *The Hero with a Thousand Faces* popularized many of Jung's theories among the American reading public.[16] The title of the book captures the message of Tarot—life is a multifaceted, ever-changing journey. The Tarot shows there are times when we display the attributes of a carefree fool. At other times, or even at the same time at a different level, our psyche displays the characteristic of an imperial, wise king, or a gracious, loving mother, a hermit, a magician, and/or a crone. The Tarot points to the potential of psychic death, destruction, judgment, and rebirth. At each moment of our life we are a complex of a thousand faces. It helps make us aware that, consciously or unconsciously, we constantly choose among them. The Tarot does not provide clear, unambiguous answers or predictions. It helps one understand that, just as change is the only constant of material reality, one's psyche is also in continual process.[17] Our challenge is to learn vigilant awareness in order to tap into the clues from our unconscious.

Elder Tales

Stories of gods and goddess from ancient cultures provide symbols for understanding the ineffable forces within ourselves and our world. Stories from modern religions metaphorically tell of various interpretations of God's plan for our lives. Fairy tales, handed down from generation to generation, are another repository of human wisdom. They do not tell of the divine, but are stories about the travails and challenges of common, ordinary folk struggling with basic human dilemmas. Most fairy tales have been told so many times, over so many centuries, that the personal elements or cultural idiosyncrasies have been melded into a universal story. Such tales are surprisingly similar the world over—in Beijing, Harare, Krakow, or Detroit.

Fairy tales are not just stories about the lives of common folk, however. Though grounded in ordinary experience, they draw explicitly on fantasy. They appeal to our imaginations. That is their strength. They tell us not what is but what can be. They offer hope, optimism, a vision for the possibilities in life.

The familiar fairy tales most of us know were created for children. They are metaphors to help young people overcome the hurdles of growing up. They show that it is possible to triumph over adversity, separate from mean parents, gain independence, and establish one's self in the adult world. The message of most fairy tales is simple and powerful: once the battle to gain fortune or true love is won, the young protagonist will live happily ever after. Fairy tales contain important lessons for the young that activate the imagination, build vision, and offer hope. Although adults know that life in the "ever after" is not a static, blissful state in never-never land, nevertheless, we continue to tell the stories to our children. But what of life in the ever after?

Allan Chinen, a psychiatrist interested in adult development and aging, knows that individuals continue to grow and face tremendous personal challenges throughout their lives, particularly as they grow old. Recognizing the power of fairy tales for the young, Chinen made it a professional challenge to see if there were any that relate truths about growing old instead of growing up. He read over four thousand fairy tales from different cultures around the world and found that many of them featured old people, but always in secondary roles. The old people in these tales did not grow or change with the story. They represented a single, immutable human trait. For example, the wicked witch in Snow White embodies unequivocal evil, and the good fairy in Pinocchio represents pure goodness. But Chinen found a handful of fairy tales, about 2 percent (approximately eighty out of four thousand), that depicted an elder as the primary protagonist confronting the developmental tasks found in the second half of life. *In the Ever After* is Chinen's collection and analysis of fifteen of these "elder tales," and it offers a compelling vision from different cultures of what life *can* be in the middle and later years. Although elder tales are most commonly found in Eastern cultures, here is one from Italy.[18]

The Shining Fish

Once upon a time, an old man and his wife lived in a house overlooking the sea. The man had been a fisherman in his youth, but with old age he could no longer fight the wind and tides and now earned his living by gathering fallen wood in a nearby forest and selling it for firewood in the village. Through the years, he and his wife gave birth to three sons, who became fishermen like their father. But all the sons drowned in storms at sea, leaving the couple alone and impoverished in old age.

One day while working in the wilderness, the old man met a stranger with a long white beard. "I know all about your troubles," the stranger said, "and I want to help." He gave the old man a small leather bag, and when the old man looked in it, he stared in astonishment. The purse was filled with gold! By the time the old man looked up, the stranger was gone. The old man threw away his wood and rushed joyously home. But along the way, he began to think. "If I tell my wife about this money, she will waste it all, spending it on relatives and friends. She will squander a fortune on useless things." So when the old man arrived at home, he said nothing to his wife. Instead, he hid the money under a pile of manure.

The next day, the old man awoke to find that his wife had cooked a wonderful breakfast, with sausages and bread. "Where did you find the money for this?" he asked his wife.

"You did not bring any wood to sell yesterday," she said, "so I sold the manure to the farmer down the road." The old man ran out, but sure enough, there was no manure, and no gold. He dared not tell his wife what happened but glumly went to work in the forest.

Deep in the woods, he met the stranger again. The stranger laughed, "I know what you did with the money, but I still want to help." So he gave the old man another purse filled with gold. The old man rushed home, but along the way he started thinking again. "If I tell my wife, she will squander this fortune. . . . Well, maybe she won't." He went back and forth in his mind, and decided to think further before telling his wife about the fortune. So he hid the money under the ashes in the fireplace. The next day he awoke to find his wife had cooked another hearty breakfast. "You did not bring back any firewood," she explained, "so I sold the ashes to the farmer down the road."

The old man ran to look, but there were no ashes or gold coins in the fireplace. In deep misery, he went back into the forest, and met the stranger a third time. The man with the long beard smiled sadly. "It seems you are not destined to be rich," the stranger said. "But I still want to help." He offered the old man a large bag. "There are frogs in this sack. Sell them in the village. Then use the money to buy the largest fish you can find—not dried fish, shellfish, sausages, cakes, or bread. Just the largest fish!" With that the stranger vanished.

The old man hurried to the village and sold his frogs. Once he had the money in hand, he saw many wonderful things he could buy at the market, and he thought the stranger's advice odd. But the old man heeded the stranger, went to the fishmonger's stall, and bought the largest fish he could find. He returned home, carrying the fish on his back.

By then evening had arrived, and with it came a storm. Rain poured down and waves pounded the beach. When the old man entered his house and gave his wife the fish, she said, "It's too late to clean the fish today. It will be dark soon." So the old man looked for a place to keep the fish. Finally, he hung it outside from the rafters. He and his wife went to bed, saying a prayer for any fishermen who might be caught at sea, like their own three sons.

In the middle of the night, someone pounded on the door. "Who could that be?" the old man and woman exclaimed, because the storm still raged outside. They opened the door and found a group of young fishermen dancing and singing. "Thank you for saving our lives!" they told the old man.

"What do you mean?" the old man asked. So the fishermen explained that they were caught at sea by the storm and did not know which way to row until the old man put out a light for them. "A light?" he asked. So they pointed. And the old man saw his fish hanging from the rafters, shining with such a great light it could be seen for miles around.

From that day on, the old man hung out the shining fish each evening to guide the young fishermen home, and they in turn shared their catch with him. And so he and his wife lived in comfort and honor the rest of their days.[19]

As with dreams and ancient myths, the imagery is strong and highly symbolic. Most elder tales begin with an old man, an old woman, or an old couple (which represents both male and female characteristics within the individual) in poverty. This poverty does not necessarily indicate a physical condition, but rather a psychological state of loss and decline. The person is losing or has lost what he or she previously valued—beauty, strength, intellectual agility, peer acclaim, friends. In the "Tale of the Shining Fish" the couple has sustained the most grievous loss imaginable, the death of their children. This can mean the actual loss of children, or it can symbolize the focus of a person's energies to this point in life—traditionally a profession for a man, and home and family for a woman. As one grows older, the sense of loss is real and must not be ignored or glossed over.

Most elder tales take place at the edge of the forest or near a body of water. This story contains both; for folklorists, Jungians, and transpersonal psychologists, bodies of water and deep forests symbolize the unconscious. The boundaries between the conscious and unconscious world surround this couple on all sides.

When gathering twigs in the forest, an elderly stranger with a long white beard gives the old man a bag of gold. At first the old man is open to the unknown and accepts the gift. Yet almost immediately after he expresses surprise and joy at this unexpected treasure, he becomes suspicious that his wife might squander his newfound wealth. His suspicion not only indicates the covetousness of the old man, it shows the psychological trait of projection, whereby an individual projects onto another person undesirable characteristics that he or she harbors or fears. Such projection is very common and not necessarily destructive in the young before they develop a strong ego; however, with maturity such projections should be recognized and rejected.

The old man's hiding of the gold in a pile of manure serves as a metaphor for his cunning but warped behavior. Two times his inability to trust another and confront his own greed causes him to lose the treasure proffered by the stranger. On his third encounter with the gift bearer, however, there is a transformation. He recognizes that his habitual pattern of behavior is not working. According to Chinen, the stranger, whom the old man finally resolves to trust, symbolizes his inner self. It is an image of psychological completion and integration. On the third meeting, the stranger offers not gold—the symbol of human culture, secular life, civilization, and human consciousness, but a bag of frogs. Frogs are highly symbolic in many cultures as representing a transitional state. They are figures of transformation. Although tempted to trade the frogs for some of the wonders at the market, the old man follows the advice of the stranger and purchases the largest fish he can find. He is laying claim symbolically to the undeveloped impulses that lie buried deep in the unconscious, as well as the urge for spiritual renewal. (In early Christianity the fish was the symbol for Christ.)

The conclusion of this tale is one of the most compelling in all folk literature. On returning home the old man and woman, too tired to clean the fish that night, found that there was not room to store it inside their cottage (inside themselves). They hung it outside, exposed to the elements, and, thinking of their sons, prayed for others who might be lost at sea before they went to bed. That shining fish, hung on the rafters of the old couple's porch, became the salvation for a group of young fishermen foundering at sea in a ravaging storm. The old man's fish from that time on was a guiding light for others. When the gift of transformation in old age is realized, it must not be hidden, but given back so as to lead others into the light.

Letting Go

The fourth step in Baker and Wheelwright's prescription for aging, detailed above, is letting go. Years ago when I was going through a period of personal crisis, I listened to a Jack Kornfield tape on meditation. The words of this American-born Buddhist still come to me when I begin to slip into a frame of mind that says it does not matter, I do not matter—a hazardous attitude, especially for older people confronted with many cultural reinforcements of this message. Kornfield says that when negative thoughts take over his consciousness, he calms himself in meditation, acknowledges his depression, and says these words: "Well, here you are again." He talks to his depression and makes a simple but profound observation that he is not his depression. He is something much more than this particular mood. His depression is a passing state of mind that, when consciously recognized, he can let pass. Many times we unconsciously form attachments to negative thoughts that take over our conscious reality and ruin our lives. There is a danger of getting stuck in one mood, wearing one face, assuming a negative attitude, and not pulling out all the potential that lies within. Many of our problems today are not caused by errors from the past, but by the way we live the realities of our life today. To move on we have to let go.

During my research into body perceptions among older women, I talked with Gay. At the time of the interview, she was eighty-two years old, living alone in a one-bedroom apartment on the top floor of a partially subsidized apartment complex for the elderly. Although a social service delivered meals to a community dining room in the building, Gay preferred to shop for her own meals and ate alone in her own apartment.

She grew up in Madison, Wisconsin, during the Depression. She has one sister, seven years older than she, and two brothers twelve and fifteen years younger. As a girl she loved sports and participated in competitive swimming. Her coach wanted her to go to Chicago to train when she was in high school, but her parents would not agree to her leaving home. Before she married in 1940, at the age of twenty-three, she attended the University of Wisconsin sporadically but never got her degree. Her mother died three months after she was married, and Gay assumed the total responsibility of raising her younger brothers, who came to live with her and her husband. Gay has two sons, the first born when she was twenty-six.

Her husband did well professionally, and they had "lovely" homes. She said she was good at cooking and entertaining. When she divorced her husband in 1964, she was living in Texas. She did not want to keep anything from the marriage and gave everything to Goodwill, a charity agency. Although Gay moved a number of times to various jobs during the next twenty years, because she has good organizational and secretarial skills, she easily found employment.

In the late 1980s, she was working at a job she enjoyed in a recreational center in California when her youngest brother offered to buy her a condo in Palm Springs, where she could retire near him. She moved to the condo, but within the year the relationship with her brother deteriorated, so she moved to Memphis to be near her oldest son. Two years ago she had a slight heart attack, and her heartbeat was so slow the doctors put in a pacemaker.

She now has little energy to do the things she would like to do. Gay enjoys her grandchildren, reading, playing cards with friends, and making quilts (by herself—she does not want to join a quilting group). She recently started writing what she calls "little stories" about her younger years.

A Word Portrait of Gay

How do I feel? I am tired. I am hurt. My heart keeps going through erratic beats with the aid of a pacemaker. It nearly stopped a year ago—beatings taken through the years have worn it down. I have always been so strong, but now am so tired, so very tired.

I can't stop now. What would happen if I just let go? Those others down in the dining room so pitiful, so repulsive, so helpless, so inhuman. They sit and stare and drool with vacant eyes. Not for me. I will hold on. My dignity is my life.

I was the apple of my daddy's eye, the whimsical muse of my mother's fancy. I lived my name in early years. Lithe limbs and big feet, I loved my body. It carried me through the water, an unencumbered stretch.

Looking back through the lenses of these aging eyes, I was secure in my parents' world—the girl who would be boy.

When a boy child came, my Dad was so happy I was afraid I would lose his affection. I had to stay on top—I became a different star, a twelve-year-old handmaiden star, hanging diapers between "rounders" (a type of baseball game).

I was good, so good that three years later when a second boy child arrived, he was mine to name. I named him Don.

Death came to my mother when the boys were in their teens; my father followed soon thereafter. The last request of each to me was "take care of our boys." I did. I raised those boys.

I was married by then. We had two boys of our own. I was a capable wife. I created a good home. My marriage ended twenty some years later when he found the type of woman he wanted. Oh, he thought I was a remarkable person, but he wanted a femme fatale with a tiny waist and little feet. Goodwill was the recipient of all those years—if he doesn't want me, I don't want anything his money bought me.

Now alone, who am I? Just who am I? I am strong, I am competent, I am dependable. I know how to please, I am the perfect helpmate. I know how to serve. Finding a job was never a problem—just don't promote me, I'll run.

Life is funny. What was I running from? Success? But what is success?

I feel I am nothing without relationships, yet I have lived alone for over thirty years. I really couldn't live with anyone.

In Santa Rosa I finally felt secure. My boy Don enticed me to leave. He bought me a condo in Palm Springs near to him, then turned his back. I feel betrayed.

How could Don betray me? He lured me in and threw me out. Why? Does he realize what has happened? Does it matter? I gave him everything. I gave him my life. I was happy when he was there.

He was mine, though born of my mother, he was mine—my parents gave him to me.

I am tired. I am hurt. Yet I find such pleasure in others and I give pleasure to others. Friends enjoy my company. I love a good joke.

I bring reconciliation to my son's family. My grandchildren adore me.

But I cannot let go of a hurt that permeates and shapes my every breath.

Why? Why? Why? It is so tiring. I am surprised to have lived so long. Getting old is scary.

After I completed Gay's word portrait, it was hard for me to share it with her, but that was the agreement I had made with everyone I interviewed. I wanted to make sure I captured their experience, not my interpretation. When Gay read her portrait, she was deeply appreciative. I had heard her story. I merely listened; I did not try to fix it. She told me she was profoundly grateful. Does this not underscore the importance of listening and relating to the whole person? Perhaps Gay's heart trouble is not all biophysical. I deeply empathized with her and her inability to let go. The maternal (Demeter) impulse for attachment held her captive. Though Don was her "adopted" child and had severed his relationship to her, Gay could not let go of what she hoped from him, even though she knew it was ruining her life.

A Personal Reflection

I am awestruck when I consider the astounding legacy of faith, imagination, and courage that individuals and communities created through the ages and passed on to me. We are surrounded by our inheritance from the past. What shall we pass on?

Caught in the eternal cycle of life, now approaching old age, I do not despair, but rejoice with the knowledge of the continual rebirth of life throughout eternity. I am part of the cycle, gifted with consciousness that gives me awareness of myself as an individual entity in this particular place and time. Though I have a specific name, a separate shape, and a particular history, I am part of a larger truth with eternal existence. I will continue. I know not in what form or spirit, but the essence of life that I inherited and enjoy will continue. Human success in unraveling many of the mysteries of matter brings us no closer to unraveling the greatest mystery—that of life. Religious practices the world over are founded on people's awareness of the spiritual reality that is an essential part of being, which goes beyond intellectual comprehension. So as I continue on this uncharted path into old age, my greatest hope is that through vigilant awareness I receive glimmers of my connections with the unfathomable mysteries of life.

7

Aging from the Inside Out

The question is not the meaning of old age, but knowing old age matters. The secret for creative aging is the realization that life, all of life, is a mysterious gift that matters. How one values that gift, regardless of age or state, is an individual choice and often a daunting challenge. In an antiaging culture, it is very easy to feel a victim of time—to believe old age is worthless and to despair for lost youth. Yet with the ever increasing "graying" of the world, today's elders are the experts who will write the script for meaningful old age. They are building a new awareness of self and society that moves beyond past expectations and assumptions. They know that aches, pains, and loss are part of life but do not define life. These elders are finding meaning through the realization that all of life matters. They know that their very being is grounded in the constant choices they, as individuals, make. Their attitude, spiritual openness, new learning, diet, exercise, activities, and companionship all *matter*.

They have learned that there is no such thing as a typical old person. Only by looking deep within themselves are they finding their own answers for personal growth into old age. These are the elders that are creating a new vision of aging that embraces the wonder of living fully in mind, body, and spirit for the whole of life.

The New Meaning of Aging

A recent full-page ad in the *Wall Street Journal* displayed an attractive, middle-aged couple, full of satisfaction and contentment, stretched out on two beach chairs contemplating their retirement. The ad was promoting financial services that would assure this idyllic future—the consummate American dream. Even though current political and economic conditions are forcing a reevaluation of the way to achieve this blissful vision, the retirement dream itself has strong appeal. In today's world of instant communication and information overload, work and stress have become synonymous. A sublime, unfettered, undemanding retirement of unstructured time is the dream of most overscheduled, overstressed, working adults. They want to free themselves from being slaves to the clock, from trying to find twelve additional hours in a twenty-four-hour day. They long to be free from continual fragmentation from obligation overload.

Freedom from relentless demands on one's time may be the dream of the middle-aged adult, but the reality of retirement (and stepping into old age) is that this freedom means that one is entirely responsible for how one spends one's time—time that may often hang heavily. When individuals are working, the demands on their time, though stressful, automatically develop most of the plots for their lives. They are part of the action—others depend on them. What they do has value to others. It does not take many months into the retirement dream to realize that what looked like paradise is just another phase of living, with new and unanticipated challenges. Retirees must create the action themselves. Without structure and relationships from external obligations, it becomes very easy to feel that the way one spends one's time really does not matter. Once into retirement it is very easy for a person to question the value of what he or she does. This is a profound dilemma for retirees, who grow old in a culture that evaluates personal worth on the basis of individual productivity and/or service to others. The huge challenge for our aging population is, can we create a viable definition for meaning and value for life in old age?

Fortunately, some of the experts who study aging are currently changing their views about old age. The twentieth century portrayed aging as a devastating problem and defined old age as an incurable disease. Today, at the beginning of the twenty-first century, research tells a different story. Although well-entrenched cultural myths and antiaging promises continue to shape perceptions and behavior in our society, new evidence is challenging past perceptions. The previously mentioned, extensive ten-year study of aging by Rowe and Kahn in the 1990s provides definitive data aimed at dispelling two of the most damaging popular myths about old age: first, that aging is pathology, and second, that you must choose your parents wisely in order to age well.

Rowe and Kahn's findings clearly demonstrate that aging men and women are not victims of problems beyond their control. As discussed in earlier chapters, aging, per se, is not an illness, and less than one-third of aging characteristics are heritable. Yet until these powerful myths are dispelled, there will continue to be an ever-increasing scramble to find biochemical "cures" for aging. Old people, resigned to what they believe to be their inevitable fate, will feel victimized by forces beyond their control and continue to look to experts for the "cure." Demonstrating that aging is truly multidimensional, Rowe and Kahn believe that individuals are primarily responsible for their own old age and find the dominant type of behavior that encourages dependency counterproductive.[1] The choices people make, the responsibility they assume for their own well-being, the way they live—how they avoid illness, what they eat and drink, their daily activities, their exercise patterns, their relationships, their mental stimulation, the routines they establish, the challenges they undertake—are the essential components for aging successfully.

David Snowdon, the University of Kentucky neurology professor who founded a three-decade-long research project of 180 nuns to determine causes of Alzheimer's and other brain diseases, as well as mental and physical disabilities associated with old age, found that the most distinguishing characteristic of the nuns who aged well was their positive attitude. All of the nuns in the study had approximately the same medical care and ate the same food, but consistently the nuns who aged well were those with positive personality traits, such as a sense of humor and adaptability. Even among those who were ill, those who accepted each new life challenge, including illness or disability, aged most successfully.[2]

Other recent research findings further illuminate our understanding of aging. Dr. Harold Koenig at Duke University has gathered compelling statistics showing that older people who attend church regularly are healthier than the nonreligious cohort of that population. He says one does not take up religion to be healthy—it is not a prescription drug—but faith in God and regular worship seem to enhance an older person's physical well-being. An exact correlation between religion and healthier aging would be impossible to establish, but empirical studies favor the importance of faith in the lives of those who are living well into old age. Here again, a multiplicity of factors most likely influences the overall health of the older persons in the study. Regular church attendance in addition to corporate worship will include some, if not all, of the following positive factors: fellowship, communal meals, meaningful relationships, adherence to a regular schedule, participating in service to others, recreational activities, and learning opportunities. No single factor determines one's health in old age. Aging is a multidimensional, holistic experience.

The profound realization from the findings of Rowe, Kahn, Snowdon, and Koenig (and many others) is that aging encompasses the whole person—the body, mind, and spirit. A major challenge for old age in our century, with so many people living so much longer, is to dispel the insidious influence of destructive cultural myths and create new understanding for the meaning of old age in the ongoing cycle of life. In many ways this challenge rests squarely with the elders themselves—a daunting challenge.

When we are old, the world around us, our physical situation, and our relationships create the stage, but we each write our own script. Guidance is helpful, but ultimately we each must find our own meaning. From those first wobbly steps as a toddler, we have lived with challenge all our lives. Anyone who has lived more then sixty-five years has at sometime, perhaps many times, faced uncertainty, loss, frustration, boredom, disorientation, doubt, depression, even suffering. Adversity, real or perceived, is part of living. We often cannot control situations that create suffering; however, we do, consciously and unconsciously, make choices in how we view and react to every situation. We can choose not to become a victim of old age.

The New Story of Aging

Martha was eighty-nine when I interviewed her. She was born in China to missionary parents and was the youngest of three children by ten years. Her early childhood memories of playing with Chinese children in the lush walled gardens of her family's compound are very happy. She spoke the language of her playmates and her Chinese nursemaid. She was seven years old when life in this secure haven came to an abrupt end. Her father became ill, and the family returned to the United States for his treatment. She has a vivid memory of other children making fun of her when she spoke Chinese. Hurt and confused, she never again ventured to speak that language (which of course she regretted in later years). The family relocated in Laurel, Mississippi, where Martha lived and went to school until her senior year of high school when the family moved to Philadelphia. She completed high school and attended college in the Northeast.

Although she received a master's degree in teaching, she did not want to be a teacher, so she worked at various clerical and retail jobs until she got married. Her husband was a lawyer who worked first for the government and then as in-house counsel for a corporation, which caused them to move a number of times. She and her husband had three daughters and were living in Chicago when he drowned in a boating accident. Martha moved back to Mississippi to be near family and went to work to support herself and her girls.

After three years she moved to Memphis to teach in a private girls school and was encouraged to get a master's degree in guidance and counseling. After twelve years another independent girls school recruited her as assistant head mistress and teacher. She eventually became head of the school and served in that capacity until her retirement when she was sixty-nine years old. She continued to work at the school for the next nineteen years, helping with development and alumni work and writing the school's history.

She was living independently in her own apartment at the time of the interview and has since moved to a retirement complex, where she has her own apartment. Martha drives her own car, leads an active social life, and attends church regularly.

A Word Portrait of Martha

You are put here for a purpose, to be guided by God. You pray that you are. Prayer, daily prayer, gives me strength to get through very tough moments.

My body? I don't think I thought about it. I was pretty strong physically. I have a good life. It's one great blessing that I was strong physically. In bad times I didn't fall apart because of my faith in God. I just believe things are going to work out.

Living in China until I was seven, I was very happy in a veritable paradise. A walled compound of coconut trees, banana trees, sedan chairs, a loving Chinese *amma* while my mother taught school, created my secure world.

And then my father was ill—responsibilities of twenty-eight years of missionary work led him to a nervous breakdown. These days they would call it depression. We came home to America—he recovered, I hurt.

I felt a great difference between me and the other children. Everyone wanted to see the little girl who talked Chinese. I did not want to be different. I was hardheaded and stubborn; I never again spoke a word of Chinese.

How did I view my body? I never gave it a thought until I was about eleven or twelve. Sitting in church I overhead two women say, "Isn't it a shame that Martha doesn't look like her mother, such a beautiful woman."

How could this be? My father told me I was beautiful. I then knew I was ugly. I took scissors and tried to cut off my heavy eyebrows. I could do nothing about my height and red hair.

But physically I was strong. I had a lot of friends, I think I had a good time. I think I just had a normal girl time. And then we moved from Mississippi to Philadelphia. I was furious, really upset. I nearly died. I was leaving all my friends.

I came to know Philadelphia was a wonderful place to live. My senior year in high school I went to a very good school. I was challenged; it was rough. There were a lot of nice girls. And I learned to play field hockey.

When I was rejected at my first choice for college, I was mad—my scores were good. I went to Hood and had a great time, lots to do and some good friends. I didn't have a really close boyfriend but didn't sit around and cry about it. I played hockey. I loved hockey.

I graduated during the Depression—there were no jobs. I got my master's in teaching—I didn't want to teach. I (re)met a family friend from Mississippi, "God, have you improved," were his first words. We dated, fell in love, and got married—a very nice romance.

We lived first in Washington, then Schenectady, then Chicago. Everything was going great—I was happy as could be. I had a lovely life in a park, Oak Park. I was exactly where I wanted to be.

There was a boating accident. He drowned. Our girls were nine, seven, and two, just little girls. That was a heartrending time. I never wanted to work. I wanted to be a mother—I wanted to be a wife and mother.

I went to work, for almost thirty years—I taught, counseled, and administered high school girls. Then one year when I was head mistress, I realized I wasn't having fun. I knew it was time to stop. My energy was going. If I wasn't going to enjoy it, I wasn't going to be any good at it. I left in December but was called back in May to do a variety of stuff at the school for another nineteen years. I finally retired when I was eighty-eight.

My body? I don't think I thought about it. I was pretty strong physically. I had a very strong spiritual upbringing. I draw great strength through prayer and meditation—it gives me a lot of physical and spiritual strength. I think they are connected.

I think optimism, having a very optimistic outlook on life, comes from having a spiritual life. I am getting old. I don't have the energy I used to, but I force myself to keep going, to go out when friends call. I would just shrivel up unless I do things.

The continual search for a relationship with God is probably the most important thing in my life. I try not to preach that, especially to my children. I want them to see the way I live. It puts more responsibility on me to try to live joyously and happily, not be selfish. If they can realize that I can live joyously because of my faith in God, I hope that will somehow help them with their faith.

At the time of this writing, Martha is ninety-four. She continues to attend Sunday worship regularly, serve dinner to the homeless on Thursday evenings, read good books, and maintain active connections with friends and family. I saw her recently at an afternoon gathering and commented on her radiant vitality. She laughed, saying, "Sometimes I just have to make myself get up and go. But it's always worth it." Optimism, adaptability, discipline, and faith seem to be Martha's formula for old age. Aging is a highly individualized process.

A New (and Very Old) Practice of Aging

From the time I was forty until my early sixties I ran three to five miles three or four times a week. I enjoyed the physical exertion, but I also loved what I came to call my enforced-moving meditation that quieted my mind and seemed to improve my emotional balance in a very busy time in my life. But the constant pounding of my feet on the pavement took its toll. My right knee became extremely painful; I could hardly walk, but I did not want an operation if I could avoid it. The orthopod prescribed some exercises, and I had to give up running. This was depressing. Not only did my knee hurt, but I could tell that generally all of my muscles were losing their strength and flexibility. And, too, I worried about my emotional stability with the loss of my "enforced meditation."

My son suggested I try yoga. I started attending weekly classes with little hope for improving my physical condition; I just wanted to ward off further stiffening and pain in my joints. It did not take long for me to realize I was gaining far more than the physical therapy for which I originally signed up. I gradually began to experience, not just to theorize about, the deep interconnections of my body, mind, and spirit. Yoga's gifts for increasing my emotional stability, as well as refreshing my spirit, were an unanticipated lagniappe.

I was fortunate that Lou Hoyt, a master teacher and delightful woman, was my instructor. Having done intensive training with B. K. S. Iyengar in India (who fifty years ago introduced yoga into the United States), as well as focused personal practice and training in the United States, Lou provided exquisitely grounded direction through firm but gentle guidance. Within the last few years, yoga has become extraordinarily popular in the United States. A rolled-up yoga mat over one's shoulder seems to have become a middle-class status symbol. But its popularity will not negate its power if its profound message is well understood. I hope others attending the many classes throughout the land, from shopping malls to church basements, are being exposed to well-grounded instruction. Yoga can be a valuable guide for holistic aging. As a science, yoga is a body of knowledge, based on observation and experimentation, systematically arranged, that illustrates attributes needed for successful aging—awareness, discipline, and continued learning.

Mr. Iyengar, who is still teaching today past the age of eighty-seven, emphasizes that yoga is not a religion or dogma. It is a philosophical and scientific inquiry documented over 2,500 years ago in the *Yoga Sutras* by Patanjali, the father of yoga. Yoga is an exploration into the nature of being with universal, timeless application, as relevant today as when first written. The *Yoga Sutras* teach people how to respond to the stresses of life and to deal with the fear and anxiety that arise throughout life and stultify and damage the body and spirit. Based on a profound knowledge of the human condition and the realization that the rules of nature are impersonal, implacable, and unbendable, yoga teaches one how to work along with nature to experience the essence of life. For example, "Yoga does not look on greed, violence, sloth, excess, pride, lust, and fear as ineradicable forms of original sin that exist to wreck our happiness. . . . They are seen as natural, if unwelcome, manifestations of the human disposition and predicament that are to be *solved*, not suppressed or denied."[3] As a lifetime journey of disciplined practice requiring zealous persistence and absolute commitment, "Yoga releases the creative potential of Life . . . by establishing a structure for self-realization, by showing how we can progress along the journey, and by opening a sacred vision of the Ultimate, of our Divine Origin, and final Destiny. The Light that Yoga sheds on life is something special. It is transformative. It does not just change the way we see things; it transforms the person who sees."[4]

In yoga, attention is first directed to the physical aspects of the body. In class students learn to give refined attention (even when it hurts a little) to the details of their physical parts as they seek to align their bones, open their joints, activate and strengthen unused muscles, and stretch other muscles that have hardened or begun to atrophy. Their intellects are activated in new ways through learning to focus on and quietly observe the energizing, life-giving quality of breath as it travels throughout all the nooks and crannies of being. Yoga helps them appreciate that mind is not localized and limited within the brain and that intelligence and memory reside throughout all the cells of the entire body. Students become aware of embodied fears that prevent them from pushing the boundaries of their comfort zones in a difficult pose and realize that they are holding on to an ingrained sense of security, which prevents them from testing or achieving a new position of balance. Intellectually and emotionally they observe the difficulty of stilling their minds in open receptivity. Thoughts continually dance through their heads in what the yogi calls a "monkey mind," trying to distract them from the quiet repose of meditation and enlarged consciousness. When they are able to quiet their minds and subdue their egos, they begin to experience the gift of the spirit that flows not only through a single body but through all bodies within the group, as they quietly settle into the resting pose of *Śavāsana* after a rigorous session. At the end of class, when they put their palms together and nod *Namaste,* an acknowledgment that the spirit within one is greeting the spirit within the other, their hearts are open. The root of the word *courage* is heart. Courage is a metaphor for inner strength, and inner strength is the mantra for aging successfully. The strength to live a vital and fulfilling old age comes from within.

Of course, speaking from personal experience, the next day after class, when my muscles are so sore I can barely get out of bed, I momentarily question the gifts of my practice, but after a couple of stretches and my morning coffee, I reflect that this is no different from the temporary discomfort I felt many times in my youth when I embarked on a new exercise regime. I consider how inflexible and tied in knots both physically and emotionally I might be without yoga and know this is part of my journey.

Although an individual may not become a practitioner of yoga, the lessons from the practice and the *Yoga Sutras* are a powerful guide for the inward journey that invites one to explore and integrate various aspects of being as one ages. Yoga, through vigilant awareness, promotes growth in mind, body, and spirit throughout the whole of life.

Our cultural assumption that old age is some kind of incurable disease rather than a natural, although limiting, process that holds great potential for growth and happiness must be resisted as a defeat and insult to our total being. Such an assumption puts us all in a hope-less struggle against the natural cycles of life and death, and we fail to appreciate the unique and mysterious gifts to be found in the whole of life.[5]

Notes

Chapter One. The Starting Point

1. Waneen W. Spirduso, *Physical Dimensions of Aging* (Champaign, Ill.: Human Kinetics, 1995), 33.

2. Charles T. Tart, *Waking Up: Overcoming the Obstacles to Human Potential* (Boston: Shambhala, 1986).

3. Jere Daniel, "Learning to Love (Gulp!) Growing Old," *Psychology Today* 27 (September–October 1994). Available online at http://www.psychologytoday.com/articles/pto-19940901-000027.html. Quoting B. Levy and E. Langer. "Aging Free from Negative Stereotypes: Successful Memory in China and among the American Deaf," *Journal of Personality and Social Psychology* 66, 989–97.

4. William A. Sadler, Ph.D., *The Third Age: Six Principles for Growth and Renewal after Forty* (Cambridge, Mass.: Perseus Books, 2000), 4.

5. Robert C. Atchley, "Continuity Theory, Self and Social Structure," in *The Self and Society in Aging Processes*, ed. Carol D. Ryff, Ph.D., and Victor W. Marshall, Ph.D. (New York: Springer, 1999), 94–121.

6. Susan Heidrich, Ph.D., R.N., "Older Women's Lives through Time," in *Advances in Nursing Science* 20, no. 3 (March 1998): 65–75.

7. Zenkei Blanche Hartman, "Beginner's Mind" (2001), available online at http://www.intrex.net/chzg/hartman4.htm.

8. Max Van Manen, *Researching Lived Experience: Human Science for an Action Sensitive Pedagogy* (Albany: State University of New York Press, 1990). Naturalistic inquiry is a method developed to understand inductively and holistically human experience in context-specific settings. It is a dynamic process-orientation method, that replaces the fixed protocol/outcome emphasis of a *controlled* experiment. Such dynamic evaluation is not tied to a single predetermined goal or outcome but focuses on the actual operations and impacts of an experience or process over a period of time. According to Michael Patton, professor of Qualitative Research, Union Institute and University ("The Nature of Research and the Paradigms Debate," *Research Voices*, 1998), categories or dimensions of analysis emerge from open-ended observations as the researcher comes to understand the patterns that exist in the empirical world under study. The research focuses on questions rather than hypotheses. In naturalistic inquiry, as contrasted to quantitative methods, the researcher

attempts to understand the multiple interrelationships among dimensions that emerge from the data without making prior assumptions or specifying hypotheses about linear or correlative relationships among narrowly defined, operationalized variables.

9. Joan Borysenko, Ph.D., *A Woman's Book of Life: The Biology, Psychology, and Spirituality of the Feminine Life Cycle* (New York: Riverhead, 1996), 94–96.

10. D. Patrick Miller, "Ending My Religion," *The Sun* 316 (April 2002). Available online at http://www.thesunmagazine.org/Miller316.pdf., 15.

11. Paul Shepard's words from *The Only World We've Got: A Paul Shepard Reader* (San Francisco: Sierra Club, 1996), 178.

12. David Brooks, in his recent book about late twentieth-century American society, says my generation nurtured self-control above all else. *Bobos in Paradise: The New Upper Class and How They Got There* (New York: Simon & Schuster, 2000).

13. Paul Tillich, *Systematic Theology*, vol. 2 (Chicago: University of Chicago Press, 1957), 10–12, also *Courage to Be* (New Haven: Yale University Press, 1952).

Chapter Two. The Cultural Context

1. Thomas R. Cole, *The Journey of Life: A Cultural History of Aging in America* (New York: Cambridge University Press, 1992), 48, comments that this may have been more a cultural ideal than a reality, as empirical data from the period is scarce.

2. U.S. Census Bureau, January 18, 2005. www.census.gov.

3. *Health, United States, 2004, with Chartbook on Trends in the Health of Americans* (Hyattsville, Md.: National Center for Health Statistics, 2004), Table 27. Available online at http://www.cdc.gov/nchs/hus.htm.

4. Richard M. Eisler and Michel Hersen, eds., *Handbook of Gender, Culture, and Health* (Mahwah, N.J., Lawrence Erlbaum Associates, 2000), 406.

5. Robert C. Atchley, *Social Forces and Aging: An Introduction to Social Gerontology*, 8th ed. (Belmont, Calif.: Wadsworth, 1997), 25–26.

6. Peter A. Diamond, David C. Lindeman, and Howard Young, *Social Security: What Role for the Future?* (Washington, D.C.: National Academy of Social Insurance, 1996).

7. Atchley, *Social Forces and Aging*, 23. Dr. Atchley points out that the only valid use of the *aged dependency ratio* is in conjunction with the *youth dependency ratio*, the ratio of the number of youths under fifteen to the total number of employable age (fifteen to sixty-four), suggesting that in the United States, eighteen would be a more accurate break point for the age between the two ratios. For an accurate picture of economic dependency, the youth and aged dependency ratios must be combined for a *total dependency ratio*. Countries with high birth rates, rather than aged populations, tend to have greater dependency burdens.

8. Steven D. Levitt and Stephen J. Dubner, *Freakonomics: A Rogue Economist Explores the Hidden Side of Everything* (New York: William Morrow, 2005), 77–79. Interestingly, Hispanics were the other type that were discriminated

against in the early part of the game on a perception (not based on fact) that they did not have adequate knowledge (information) to answer the questions correctly. No discrimination was found against African Americans or females. Levitt conjectured that a possible reason is that so much publicity has been given to the prejudice against those two groups of people that their elimination would imply bigotry on the part of the other contestant.

9. John W. Rowe, M.D., President, Mount Sinai Hospital and Medical School, and Robert L. Kahn, Ph.D., Professor of Psychology and Public Health, University of Michigan, identified these myths in their book *Successful Aging* (New York: Pantheon, 1998), after a ten-year study funded by the McArthur Foundation.

10. Charles Alexander and Ellen Langer, *Higher Stages of Human Development* (New York: Oxford University Press, 1990).

11. Barry D. McPherson, *Aging as a Social Process: An Introduction to Individual and Population Aging* (Toronto: Butterworths, 1983), 376.

12. Priscilla Ebersole and Patricia Hess, *Toward Healthy Aging: Human Needs and Nursing Response* (St. Louis: Mosby Publishers, 1998), 6.

13. Cole, *The Journey of Life*, xx. Cole's book is a highly readable, comprehensively researched book on attitudes and cultural beliefs toward aging throughout the nation's history.

14. Susan M. Heidrich and Carol D. Ryff, "Physical and Mental Health in Later Life: The Self-System as Mediator," *Psychology and Aging* 8, no. 3 (1993): 327.

15. Gail Sheehy, *Passages: Predictable Crisis of Adult Life* (New York: E.P. Dutton, 1976).

16. Lenard W. Kaye and Jordan I. Kosberg, eds., *Elderly Men: Special Problems and Professional Challenges* (New York: Springer, 1997).

17. Erik H. Erikson, *Identity and the Life Cycle* (International Universities Press, 1959). Various adaptations of Erikson's theory give slightly different ages to the specific stages, but the developmental issues are the same. See http://psychology.about.com (search for Erikson's developmental theory). It is interesting that Carol Hren Hoare, in her book *Erikson on Development in Adulthood: New Insights from the Unpublished Papers* (New York: Oxford University Press, 2002), concludes, after reading all of Erikson's writings, published and unpublished, that he was not as tied to the adult-stage theory of human development as many of his followers advocated.

18. Simone de Beauvoir's *The Coming of Age*, trans. Patrick O'Brian (New York: W. W. Norton, 1996), written in 1970, is a comprehensive survey of cultural perceptions of old age and treatment of old people in Western history and other cultures.

19. Kenneth J. Gergen, "The Turning Point in Life-Span Study," chap. 4 in *Toward Transformation of Social Knowledge*, 2nd ed. (London: Sage Publications, 1994). After Gergen gives a number of case studies illustrating how it is impossible to predict adult development from child behavior (Adolf Hitler was a sensitive, artistic, well-behaved child; Mahatma Gandhi, in an

autobiographical account called himself a coward; and Charles Wilson, who became a ruthless killer in the Manson gang, was a well-adjusted, middle-class, church-going, popular kid), he sites numerous studies that systematically examined individuals as they developed over time. Looking at various traits measured during infancy, and the same traits as assessed over the thirty-year-old period, there were virtually no significant findings.

20. Ibid., 157.

Chapter Three. Beyond Patriarchy

1. Fundamentalist sects exist today in the United States that adhere to the complete subjugation of women and promote teenage brides and multiple marriage by the males, even though it is clearly against the law. See Jon Krakauer, *Under the Banner of Heaven: A Story of Violent Faith* (New York: Doubleday, 2003).

2. Mary Daly, *Beyond God the Father: Towards a Philosophy of Women's Liberation,* 2nd ed. (Boston: Beacon Press, 1985), is a classic in this area. See also Rosemary Radford Ruether, ed., *Religion and Sexism: Images of Women in the Jewish and Christian Traditions* (New York: Simon & Schuster, 1974); Riane Eisler, *The Chalice and the Blade: Our History, Our Future* (New York: Harper-Collins, 1987); and Judith Plaskow and Carol Christ, *Weaving the Visions, New Patterns in Feminist Spirituality* (San Francisco: HarperSanFrancisco, 1989).

3. A historical scrutiny of three of the four major religions of the world, Christianity, Buddhism, and Islam, reveals a strong androcentric bias and patriarchal practice. See Rita M. Gross, *Buddhism after Patriarchy: A Feminist History, Analysis, and Reconstruction of Buddhism* (Albany: State University of New York Press, 1993); Yvonne Yazbeck Haddad and John L. Esposito, eds., *Islam, Gender, and Social Change* (New York: Oxford University Press, 1998). Hinduism, where religious values are often expressed in terms of feminine imagery and female divinities, is the exception. See Subhadra Mitra Channa, "Globalization and Modernity in India: A Gendered Critique," in *Urban Anthropology and Studies of Cultural Systems and World Economic Development* 33, no. 1 (2004): 37–71.

4. Barbara Brown Taylor, *The Luminous Web: Essays on Science and Religion* (Cambridge, Boston: Cowley Publications, 2000).

5. Sandra Scham, "The Lost Goddess of Israel," *Archaeology* 58, no. 2 (March/April 2005); William H. Dever, *Did God Have a Wife? Archaeology and Folk Religion in Ancient Israel* (Grand Rapids, Mich.: Wm. B. Eerdmans, 2005).

6. Rosemary Radford Ruether, *Women and Redemption: A Theological History* (Minneapolis: Fortress Press, 1998).

7. Barbara Walker, *The Crone: Woman of Age, Wisdom, and Prayer* (San Francisco: HarperSanFrancisco, 1985), 142.

8. Other contemporary English dictionaries (Merriam-Webster's Online Dictionary, 10th ed.; *Compact Oxford Dictionary; Cambridge International Dictionary of English; Wordsmyth English Dictionary;* and *Cambridge Dictionary of*

American English) give the same definition of *hag*: "an ugly old woman, especially a vicious or malicious one."

9. The meaning of *hag* as "an ugly old woman" is traced to the medieval usage of *hagge* in *Piers the Plowman*, written about 1394. However, when I searched in a copy of the original text of this book, I found the word *hag* was used only once. Buried deeply in the text, it was used in a description of a covetous old courtier (male): "he had two bleared eyes, like a blind *hag*." The word *hag* is found in the text, but the meaning inferred seemingly came from contemporaneous understanding.

10. Lu Gwei-Djen and Joseph Needham, *Science and Civilisation in China* ed. Nathan Sivin, (New York: Cambridge University Press, 2004).

11. Daniel J. Siegel, M.D., *The Developing Mind: Toward a Neurobiology of Interpersonal Experience* (New York: Guilford Press, 1999), 229.

Chapter Four. The Scientific Paradigm

1. René Descartes, "Meditation VI," *Great Books of the Western World* (London: Encyclopaedia Britannica, 1952).

2. Simone de Beauvoir, *The Coming of Age,* trans. Patrick O'Brian (New York: W. W. Norton, 1996), 45–80.

3. Ibid., 141.

4. Marilou Awiakta, *Selu: Seeking the Corn-Mother's Wisdom* (Golden, Colo.: Fulcrum Publishers, 1993).

5. De Beauvoir, *The Coming of Age,* 41–42.

6. Ibid., 17.

7. Charles Singer, *A Short History of Science to the Nineteenth Century* (London: Clarendon Press, 1941), 38, 41.

8. Aristotle, "On Youth and Old Age, On Life and Death, On Breathing," trans. G. R. T. Ross, *Great Books of the Western World,* ed. Robert Maynard Hutchins (London: Encyclopaedia Britannica, 1952), chaps. 6:20–8:25.

9. Henry Schuman, *Main Currents of Scientific Thought: A History of the Sciences* (New York: S. F. Mason, 1953), 181–90.

10. A. Rupert Hall, *The Revolution in Science, 1500–1750* (Boston: Addison-Wesley, 1983), 167.

11. Singer, *A Short History of Science to the Nineteenth Century,* 347.

12. Paul Starr, *The Social Transformation of American Medicine* (New York: Basic Books, 1982), 142.

13. Ibid., 135–37.

14. Ibid., 141.

15. Ibid., 113.

16. Thomas R. Cole, *The Journey of Life: A Cultural History of Aging in America* (New York: Cambridge University Press, 1992), 194–96.

17. David B. Morris, *Illness and Culture in the Postmodern Age* (Berkeley: University of California Press, 1998), 15–16.

18. Aubrey de Grey, "The War on Aging: Speculations on Some Future Chapters in the Never-ending Story of Human Life Extension," in *The Scientific*

Conquest of Death: Essays on Infinite Lifespans, ed. The Immortality Institute (Buenos Aires: Libros en Red, 2004).

19. Jean-Francois Lyotard, *The Postmodern Condition: A Report on Knowledge,* trans. Geoff Bennington and Brian Massumi (Minneapolis: University of Minnesota Press, 1993).

20. Sander Gilman, *Difference and Pathology: Stereotypes of Sexuality, Race, and Madness* (Ithaca, N.Y.: Cornell University Press, 1985), 33.

21. Morris, *Illness and Culture in the Postmodern Age,* 56.

22. Dr. Lisa Schwartz and Steven Woloshin, "Changing Disease Definitions: Implications for Disease Prevalence," *Effective Clinical Practice* (March/April 1999): 76–84.

23. Susan Kelleher and Duff Wilson, "Suddenly Sick," *Seattle Times,* June 26, 2005.

24. Alan Bonsteel, M.D., "Behind the White Coat," *The Humanist* 57 (March-April 1997): 15–18.

25. Cole explains his use of the term *institutionalization* by referring to another example of "institution" in our culture—marriage and the institution of the family—believed by many to be a fundamental base of society.

26. Cole, *The Journey of Life,* 196.

27. Robert C. Atchley, *Social Forces and Aging: An Introduction to Social Gerontology,* 8th ed. (Belmont, Calif.: Wadsworth, 1997), 89.

28. Thomas McGowan, "Ageism and Discrimination," in *Encyclopedia of Gerontology,* vol. 1 (Burlington, Mass.: Academic Press, 1996), 1–10.

29. William A. Sadler, Ph.D., *The Third Age: Six Principles for Growth and Renewal after Forty* (Cambridge, Mass.: Perseus Books, 2000), 79.

30. Atchley, *Social Forces and Aging.*

31. Waneen W. Spirduso, *Physical Dimensions of Aging* (Champaign, Ill.: Human Kinetics, 1995), 33.

32. David Sobel, M.D., regional director of Kaiser Permanente, "Keynote Address," Annual Conference of the National Institute for the Clinical Application of Behavioral Medicine, 1999, noted that attitude was even more important than exercise.

33. When used qualitatively, such as "old maid," "old fashioned," "old guard," "old witch," "old fogey," it carries a pejorative meaning, as contrasted to young and vital.

34. John W. Rowe and Robert L. Kahn, *Successful Aging* (New York: Pantheon Books, 1998).

35. Spirduso, *Physical Dimensions of Aging,* 25.

36. C. G. Jung, "On the Nature of the Psyche," in *The Structure and Dynamics of the Psyche, The Collected Works,* vol. 8, trans. R. F. C. Hull (Princeton: Princeton University Press, 1960), par. 418.

37. Leslie G. Walker, Ph.D., and Oleg Eremin, M.D., "Psychoneuroimmunology: A New Fad or the Fifth Cancer Treatment Modality?" *The American Journal of Surgery* 170 (July 1995): 2–4.

38. Quoted in William Keepin, "Lifework of David Bohm: River of Truth," originally published in *Re-vision* 16 (Summer 1993), available online at http://www.gaia.dk/International/ExternalArticles/bohm-lifework.pdf.

39. Carol D. Ryff, Ph.D., and Victor W. Marshall, Ph.D., eds., *The Self and Society in the Aging Process* (New York: Springer, 1999), 4.

40. Administrators justified outright discrimination against qualified women candidates on the grounds that they would not continue to practice after marriage. For the next half-century after 1910, except for wartime, the schools maintained quotas limiting women to about 5 percent of medical student admissions.

Chapter Five. The Threshold

1. Candace B. Pert, Ph.D., *Molecules of Emotion: The Science Behind Mind-Body Medicine* (New York: Scribner, 1997), 223.

2. Francisco Varela, "The Emergent Self," chap. 12 in John Brockman, *The Third Culture: Beyond the Scientific Revolution* (New York: Simon & Schuster, 1995), 209–22. Available online at http://www.edge.org/documents/Third-Culture/t-Ch.12.html. Varela, following the intellectual tradition of quantum physicists such as Niels Bohr and Werner Heisenberg, applied their epistemological grounding to his study in biology and the human body.

3. Evelyn Fox Keller and Helen E. Longino, eds., *Oxford Readings in Feminism: Feminism and Science* (New York: Oxford University Press, 1996). Keller, writing in 1982, believed that a feminist critique of science was occurring and saw that the extension of feminist critique of the foundations of scientific thought is the reconceptualization of objectivity as a dialectic process, so as to allow for the possibility of distinguishing the objective from the objectivist illusion. She believes that feminists should not create new science but refine the effort of understanding the world in rational terms by adding critical self-reflection.

4. Pert, *Molecules of Emotion*, 26.

5. Ibid., 184, 185.

6. The notion of an immune system initially arose within Western medicine as a concept of an internal physiological system that protects or defends our bodies against a potentially hostile (pathogenic) environment. Its appearance during the late nineteenth and early twentieth centuries coincided with the development of the germ theory of disease, and much of modern immunological language and research is still based on a metaphor that assumes powerful, warlike, hierarchical, autonomous activity. A broader view, however, is emerging from interdisciplinary studies of the relationship between immunological and psychological or sociocultural behavior. It conceives of the immune system as an integrative, cognitive system that discriminates between self and non-self and continually maintains a coherent relationship between self and context (*Social and Cultural Lives of Immune Systems,* ed. James M. Wilce Jr. [New York: Routledge, 2003], 35).

7. Pert, *Molecules of Emotion,* 18. Pert's highly readable book for the non-scientist gives a personal history of the deeply ingrained Cartesian mind-body

split in established biomedical research and in particular the prejudice and political pressure against a holistic approach to understanding the body's immune system at the National Institutes of Health in the 1980s.

8. Bruce H. Lipton, *The Biology of Belief* (Santa Rosa, Calif.: Mountain of Love/Elite Books, 2005); see also video presentation *The Biology of Perception*, (2000).

9. Humberto R. Maturana and Francisco J. Varela, *The Tree of Knowledge: The Biological Roots of Human Understanding* (Boston: Shambhala, 1987), 69.

10. Michael Kress, "Expanding Universe," *Spirituality and Health* (October 2005): 32.

11. Mary Powers, Memphis *Commercial Appeal,* August 10, 2005.

12. Stephen B. Kritchevsky, Ph.D., et al., "Angiotensi-Converting Enzyme Insertion/Deletion Genotype, Exercise, and Physical Decline," *Journal of the American Medical Association* 294, no. 6 (August 10, 2005): 691–98.

13. Richard C. Strohman, "Genetic Determinism as a Failing Paradigm in Biology and Medicine: Implications for Health and Wellness," *Journal of Social Work Education* 39 (March 2003): 169–91.

14. Ibid.

15. John A. Astin, "Why Patients Use Alternative Medicine," *Journal of the American Medical Association* 279, no. 19 (May 1998): 1548–53.

16. Peter Ellsworth, retired CEO, Sharp PPO, interview (October 1, 1999). Ellsworth observed that there has been little modification of traditional medical school curriculums in the United States, stating, "They believe they can't teach things that are not clinically and quantitatively proven by trials. The nurses are the key." The holistic approach is being incorporated in many nursing schools across the country, and practicing nurses are increasingly embracing holism.

17. Christiane Northrup, M.D., *Women's Bodies, Women's Wisdom: Creating Physical and Emotional Health and Healing,* rev. ed. (New York: Bantam, 1998), xxxi.

18. Ibid., 27. Author's emphasis.

19. Ibid., 24.

20. Margaret Talbot, "The Placebo Prescription," *New York Times Magazine* (January 9, 2000).

21. Ibid., 6–8.

22. From a presentation Dr. Loes made at the 11th annual Neuroimmunology conference of the National Institute for the Clinical Application of Behavioral Medicine, December 5, 1999, Palm Springs, California.

23. Larry Dossey, M.D., *Reinventing Medicine: Beyond Mind-Body to a New Era* (San Francisco: HarperSanFrancisco, 1999), 18–21.

24. An example Dossey gives of the limitations of Era I reductive medicine is its ineffectiveness in combating chronic and degenerative illnesses that require a holistic context to be understood.

25. Strohman, "Genetic Determinism as a Failing Paradigm."

26. "Leading the Change: Six Visions for the Future of Medicine," *Spirituality & Health* (March/April 2004): 46–47.

27. Joan Erikson, *The Life Cycle Completed: Erik H. Erikson* (New York: W. W. Norton, 1998), 114.

28. C. G. Jung, *Civilization in Transition, The Collected Works*, vol. 10, trans. R. F. C. Hull (Princeton: Princeton University Press, 1969). An excellent introduction and explication of Jung's work is Jolanda Jocobi's *The Psychology of C. G. Jung*, first published in England in 1942 by Rutledge & Kegan Paul, Ltd.; published in United States in 1943 by Yale University Press; English ed. 1973.

Chapter Six. Insights for Aging

1. P. King, "Notes on the Psychoanalysis of Older Patients," *Journal of Analytical Psychology* 19 (1974): 264. Although Freud's theories have lost sway among contemporary psychologists and counselors, their influence is still seen among many older people in America today. Contemporary cultures' preoccupation (at least according to the television ads) with erectile dysfunction fosters a belief that if a man cannot "perform" as a young man, life is over. This mind-set, grounded in Freudian theory, can create personal anxiety and prevent exploration of new ways to enjoy intimacy in later life.

2. Bruce Baker and Jane Wheelwright, "Analysis with the Aged," in *Jungian Analysis*, ed. Murray Stein (La Salle, Ill.: Open Court, 1982), 257. The idea that the old as well as the young continue to grow psychologically toward fulfillment of their psychic potentials distinguishes the Jungian approach from other therapies.

3. Jung believed there were four functions (thinking, feeling, intuitive, and sensate) or ways that people respond to their environment and process information. Although everyone has the innate capacity of all four functions, normally one is dominant and a second developed in a supportive capacity, while the other two (the inferior functions) lie dormant within an individual personality. The Myers Briggs Personality Type Indicator and Kolb Learning Style Inventory are valuable tools for determining one's primary, secondary, and inferior functions. For a fully balanced, functioning personality, a person should seek to develop the inferior functions to use all four in concert.

4. Baker and Wheelwright, "Analysis with the Aged," 266–70.

5. Carl Jung, *Two Essays on Analytical Psychology, The Collected Works*, vol. 7, trans. R. F. C. Hull, 2nd ed. (Princeton: Princeton University Press, 1967), 221.

6. The shadow side of one's personality is a basic concept of Jungian theory. Robert A. Johnson's books, such as *Owning Your Own Shadow: Understanding the Dark Side of the Psyche* (San Francisco: HarperSanFrancisco, 1993), are very helpful in explaining how to recognize one's shadow side.

7. Joan Borysenko, Ph.D., and Wayne Muller, M.Div., presentation on "Spirituality and Healing" at the 11th International Conference of The National Institute for the Clinical Application of Behavioral Medicine, December 1999, Palm Springs, California.

8. Jung, *Two Essays on Analytical Psychology, The Collected Works*, vol. 7, 238.

9. C. G. Jung, "Psychology and Literature," *The Spirit in Man, Art, and Literature, Collected Works,* vol. 15, trans. R. F. C. Hull (Bollingen Series 20, Pantheon Books, 1966), 101. "The artist is not a person endowed with free will who seeks his own ends, but one who allows art to realize its purposes through him. As a human being he may have moods and a will and personal aims, but as an artist he is 'man' in a higher sense—he is 'collective man,' a vehicle and moulder of the unconscious psychic life of mankind."

10. Richard Tomlinson, *From Mycenae to Constantinople: The Evolution of the Ancient City* (New York: Routledge, 1992), chap. 10. The author's comprehensive description of the city's ruins demonstrate the city's commercial importance and religious practices, but perhaps the most moving account is his writing on the surrounding countryside and the ancient rock burial sites, which, since the area had been cut off from evolving civilization for so long, evoked a feeling that he was truly stepping into ancient times.

11. Christine Downing, *The Goddess: Mythological Images of the Feminine* (New York: Crossroad, 1981).

12. "Demeter," from the Web site "Greek Mythology From the Iliad to the Last Tyrant: The Immortals," http://messagenet.com/myths/bios/demeter .html

13. Peter Kingsley, *In the Dark Places of Wisdom* (Inverness, Calif.: The Golden Sufi Center, 1999).

14. Dreams, recognized as a conveyer of divine truth since biblical times (most every kindergarten Sunday school hears about Joseph's interpretation of the pharaoh's dreams), are honored and used today by counselors, analysts, and spiritual leaders to ferret out the deeper meaning of individual and collective psyches. Joyce Rockwell Hudson, *Natural Spirituality: Recovering the Wisdom Tradition in Christianity* (Danielsville, Ga.: JRH Publications, 1998), is an excellent source for understanding the power of dreams.

15. Laurens van der Post, "Introduction," in Sallie Nichols, *Jung and Tarot: An Archetypal Journey* (York Beach, Me.: Samuel Weiser, 1980).

16. Joseph Campbell, *The Hero with a Thousand Faces* (Princeton: Princeton University Press, 1972).

17. Nichols, *Jung and Tarot*; and Joseph Campbell and Richard Roberts, *Tarot Revelations,* 3rd ed. (San Anselmo, Calif.: Vernal Equinox Press, 1987), are fine references for Jungian insight into the symbols of Tarot. The books of Alice O. Howell, *Jungian Synchronicity in Astrological Signs and Ages* (1990), *The Dove in the Stone: Finding the Sacred in the Commonplace,* and *The Web in the Sea: Jung, Sophia, and the Geometry of the Soul* (1993) (all Wheaton, Ill.: Quest Books), are excellent resources for Jungian symbolism in astrology and ancient geometry.

18. Allan B. Chinen, *In the Ever After: Fairy Tales and the Second Half of Life* (Wilmette, Ill.: Chiron Publications, 1989).

19. Summarized from "Shining Fish," in Italo Calvino, *Italian Folk Tales* (New York: Pantheon, 1978).

Chapter Seven. Aging from the Inside Out

1. John W. Rowe and Robert L. Kahn, *Successful Aging* (New York: Pantheon, 1998).

2. David Snowdon, Ph.D., *Aging with Grace: What the Nun Study Teaches Us about Leading Longer, Healthier, and More Meaningful Lives* (New York: Bantam, 2001).

3. B. K. S. Iyengar, *Light on Life: The Yoga Journey to Wholeness, Inner Peace, and Ultimate Freedom* (New York: Rodale, 2005), xv.

4. Ibid, xxi.

5. Bruce Baker and Jane Wheelwright, "Analysis with the Aged," in *Jungian Analysis*, ed. Murray Stein (La Salle, Ill.: Open Court, 1982), 256–73.

Selected Bibliography

The bibliography for this study represents a wide assortment of books, articles, Web sites, and creative writing from an eclectic array of resources, some very old, some just published. I believe aging, like life, is extraordinarily complex and has an unfathomable array of facets. The study of aging cannot be understood by a rifle-shot, singular approach within one discipline, even though focused, in-depth studies from the perspective of a single discipline are invaluable for shedding light on the total experience.

Within the long list of resources that I used in my research and writing, I found that a number of authors were particularly helpful. Their books were like good friends to whom I returned over and over again for insight and inspiration. My short list includes:

Atchley, Robert C. *Social Forces and Aging: An Introduction to Social Gerontology.* 8th ed. Belmont, Calif.: Wadsworth, 1997. An excellent primer for the study of human aging in the United States today.

Beauvoir, Simone de. *The Coming of Age.* Trans. Patrick O'Brian. New York: W. W. Norton, 1996. To break what she labels "the conspiracy of silence" in viewing old age, de Beauvoir did exhaustive research on how old age has been viewed over thousands of years within a multitude of cultures.

Berman, Morris. *Coming to Our Senses: Body and Spirit in the Hidden History of the West.* New York: Bantam, 1990. A comprehensive review of the subjugation of body awareness and appreciation of the physical senses within the history of Western culture.

Campbell, Joseph, ed. *The Portable Jung.* Trans. R. F. C. Hull. New York: Penguin, 1971. A general overview of Carl Jung's analytical psychology that emphasizes the importance of the spiritual dimension for understanding the human psyche and the value of metaphor, symbols, stories, and dreams for exploring the unconscious dimension of the human psyche. (Other helpful books in this area, listed below, are *Jung and Tarot* by Sallie Nichols, *In the Ever After* by Allan B. Chinen, and *Natural Spirituality* by Joyce Rockwood Hudson.)

Capra, Fritjof. *The Web of Life: A New Scientific Understanding of Living Systems.* New York: Doubleday, 1996. A description of the profound interrelationships and interdependencies of psychological, biological, physical, social, and cultural phenomena, in terms comprehensible to a nonscientific reader.

Cole, Thomas R. *The Journey of Life: A Cultural History of Aging in America.* New York: Cambridge University Press, 1992. By giving a penetrating analysis of the history of aging within the Western tradition, Cole demonstrates how cultural beliefs have shaped individual and societal attitudes about old age.

Dossey, Larry, M.D. *Reinventing Medicine: Beyond Mind-Body to a New Era of Healing.* San Francisco: HarperSanFrancisco, 1999. Dossey gives scientific and medical proof that the spiritual dimension works in healing.

Heilbrun, Carolyn G. *The Last Gift of Time: Life beyond Sixty.* New York: Ballantine Books, 1997. Heilbrun's personal story of how she realized midcareer that she must eschew the methodology of traditional "objective" scholarship, claim her own standpoint, and situate herself in her literary research and writing.

Iyengar, B. K. S. *Light on Life: The Yoga Journey to Wholeness, Inner Peace, and Ultimate Freedom.* New York: Rodale, 2005. The yoga master who introduced the practice to the United States over fifty years ago gives an inspiring and highly readable description of how yoga promotes health and well-being.

Kabat-Zinn, Jon. *Full Catastrophe Living: Using the Wisdom of Your Body and Mind to Face Stress, Pain, and Illness.* New York: Bantam, 1990. Building on Herbert Benson's seminal research on the relaxation response, Kabat-Zinn demonstrates the power of meditation and moment-to-moment awareness to counter the destructive nature of stress on our bodies and psyches.

Keller, Evelyn Fox. *A Feeling for the Organism: The Life and Work of Barbara McClintock.* The remarkable story of a Nobel Prize laureate who withstood the isolation and criticism of her peers for decades. McClintock sought to understand the function instead of the mechanism of genetic material—a holistic approach. Rather than seeking norms, she focused meticulous research and incredible patience on nature's anomalies and demonstrated the innate flexibility and adaptability of living organisms.

———, and Helen E. Longino, eds. *Oxford Readings in Feminism: Feminism and Science.* New York: Oxford University Press, 1996. The editors are feminist scholars who believe that pure, value-free objectivity is impossible and advocate reconceptualizing objectivity as a dialectic process, "to allow for the possibility of distinguishing the objective from the objectivist illusion." This collection of essays supports their belief that all scientific inquiry should be situated through rigorous, reflective analysis of the underlying value assumptions and the total (perhaps hidden) context within which the researcher operates. Donna Haraway's thesis that nature is *constructed,* not *discovered* is most provocative. Haraway's article is entitled "Situated Knowledges: The Science Question in Feminism and the Privilege of Partial Perspective," 249–63.

Maturana, Humberto R., and Francisco J. Varela. *The Tree of Knowledge: The Biological Roots of Human Understanding.* Boston: Shambhala, 1987. An explanation by award-winning biologists that evolution and natural development are not simply a response to objective reality "out there," but that the act of cognition, the process of knowing, is actively rooted in all biological structure.

Morris, David B. *Illness and Culture in the Postmodern Age.* Berkeley: University of California Press, 1998. A comprehensive analysis of the dramatic changes in medical diagnosis, treatment, and delivery systems that have transformed our culture's understanding and definition of illness.

Moustakas, Clark. *Heuristic Research: Design, Methodology, and Applications.* Newbury Park, Calif.: Sage Publications, 1990. A practical guide of how to incorporate and authenticate one's personal experience in scholarly research.

Northrup, Christiane, M.D. *Women's Bodies, Women's Wisdom: Creating Physical and Emotional Heal and Healing.* Rev. ed. New York: Bantam, 1998. This comprehensive resource book for women's health problems is an outstanding guide for holistic understanding for healing the body, mind, and spirit.

Oliver, Mary. *Winter Hours.* New York: Houghton Mifflin, 1999. Poetic inspiration for seeing life and aging through creative eyes.

Pert, Candace B., Ph.D. *Molecules of Emotion: The Science Behind Mind-Body Medicine.* New York: Scribner, 1997. A highly readable account of this molecular biologist's discovery of the opiate receptor, which created scientific evidence of a biochemical link between consciousness, mind, and body. The story of her personal struggle against the overt sexism of her profession is a remarkable testimony that demonstrates the power of exposing her personal situation in the development and reporting of scientific research.

Scott-Maxwell, Florida. *The Measure of My Days.* New York: Penguin Books, 1979. This gifted writer gives a vivid account of where she finds meaning in old age.

Taylor, Barbara Brown. *The Luminous Web: Essays on Science and Religion.* Cambridge, Mass.: Cowley, 2000. In rejecting an either/or approach for understanding our world, Taylor's beautiful explications of scientific phenomena demonstrate that we need both science *and* religion to explore the mysteries and unknowns of nature.

Additional Resources

Astin, John A. "Why Patients Use Alternative Medicine." *Journal of the American Medical Association* 279, no. 19 (May 1998): 1548–53.

Awiakta, Marilou. *Selu: Seeking the Corn-Mother's Wisdom.* Golden, Colo.: Fulcrum Publishers, 1993.

Baker, Bruce, and Jane Wheelwright. "Analysis with the Aged." In *Jungian Analysis,* ed. Murray Stein, 256–73. La Salle, Ill.: Open Court, 1982.

Benson, Herbert, M.D. "The Relaxation Response." In *Mind-Body Medicine: How to Use Your Mind for Better Health,* ed. Daniel Goleman, Ph.D., and Joel Gurin. New York: Consumer Reports Books, 1993, 233–57.

Berger, Peter L., and Thomas Luckmann. *The Social Construction of Reality: A Treatise in Sociology of Knowledge.* New York: Doubleday, 1966.

Berry, Carmen Renee. *Coming Home to Your Body: 365 Simple Ways to Nourish Yourself Inside and Out.* Berkeley: Page Mill Press, 1996.

Bleier, Ruth, ed. *Feminist Approaches to Science.* New York: Pergamon Press, 1986.

Bolen, Jean Shinoda. *Crossing to Avalon: A Woman's Midlife Pilgrimage.* San Francisco: HarperSanFrancisco, 1995.

Bonsteel, Alan, M.D. "Behind the White Coat." *The Humanist* 57 (March–April 1997): 15–18.

Bordo, Susan. *Unbearable Weight: Feminism, Western Culture, and the Body.* Berkeley: University of California Press, 1993.

———. *Gender/Body/Knowledge: Feminist Reconstructions of Being and Knowing.* New Brunswick, N.J.: Rutgers University Press, 1992.

Bortz, Walter M., M.D. *We Live Too Short and Die Too Long: How to Achieve Your Natural 100-Year-Plus Life Span.* New York: Bantam, 1992.

Borysenko, Joan, Ph.D. *A Woman's Book of Life: The Biology, Psychology, and Spirituality of the Feminine Life Cycle.* New York: Riverhead, 1996.

Brown, Barbara, Ph.D. *Bio-feedback: New Directions for the Mind.* New York: Harper & Row, 1974.

Chinen, Allan B. *In the Ever After: Fairy Tales and the Second Half of Life.* Wilmette, Ill.: Chiron Publications, 1989.

Chopra, Deepak. *Ageless Body, Timeless Mind: The Quantum Alternative to Growing Old.* New York: Harmony Books, 1993.

Daniel, Jere. "Learning to Love (Gulp!) Growing Old." *Psychology Today* 27 (September–October 1994). http://www.psychologytoday.com/articles/pto-19940901-000027.html.

Das, Lama Surya. *Awakening the Buddha Within: Tibetan Wisdom for the Western World.* New York: Broadway Books, 1997.

Delany, Sarah, and A. Elizabeth Delany, with Amy Hill Hearth. *The Delany Sisters' Book of Everyday Wisdom.* New York: Kodansha International, 1994.

Diamond, Peter A., David C. Lindeman, and Howard Young. *Social Security: What Role for the Future?* Washington, D.C.: National Academy of Social Insurance, 1996.

Dinan, Steve. "Consciousness" Timeline. 2001. http://www.enlightenment.com/media/essays/consciousnesstimeline.html.

Douglass, Bruce, and Clark Moustakas. "Heuristic Inquiry: The Internal Search to Know." *Journal of Humanistic Psychology* 25, no. 3 (1985).

Downing, Christine. *The Goddess: Mythological Images of the Feminine.* New York: Crossroad, 1981.

Dychtwald, Kenneth, Ph.D. *The Age Wave: How the Most Important Trend of Our Time Can Change Your Future.* New York: Bantam, 1990.

Ebersole, Priscilla, and Patricia Hess. *Toward Healthy Aging: Human Needs and Nursing Response.* St. Louis: Mosby Publishers, 1998.

Erikson, Erik H., Joan M. Erikson, and Helen Q. Kivnich. *Vital Involvement in Old Age.* New York: W. W. Norton, 1986.

Furman, Frida Kerner. *Facing the Mirror: Older Women and the Beauty Shop Culture.* New York: Routledge, 1997.

Gatens, Moira. *Imaginary Bodies: Ethics, Power, and Corporeality.* London and New York: Routledge, 1996.

Gaydos, H. Lea. "Three Women Healers." Ph.D. dissertation, unpublished. Cincinnati: The Union Institute, 1999.

Gergen, Kenneth J. "The Turning Point in Life-Span Study." In *Toward Transformation in Social Knowledge,* chap. 4. 2nd ed. London: Sage Publications, 1994.

Gilman, Sander. *Difference and Pathology: Stereotypes of Sexuality, Race, and Madness.* Ithaca, N.Y.: Cornell University Press, 1985.

Gimbutas, Marja Alseikaite. *The Goddess and Gods of Old Europe, 7000 to 3500 B.C.* Berkeley: University of California Press, 1990.

———. *The Language of the Goddess.* New York: Harper & Row, 1998.

Giorgi, Amadeo, ed. *Phenomenology and Psychological Research.* Pittsburgh: Duquesne University Press, 1985.

Goleman, Daniel, and Joel Gurin, eds. *Mind-Body Medicine: How to Use Your Mind for Better Health.* New York: Consumer Reports Book, 1993.

Grey, Aubrey de. "The War on Aging: Speculations on Some Future Chapters in the Never-ending Story of Human Life Extension." In *The Scientific Conquest of Death: Essays on Infinite Life Spans,* ed. The Immortality Institute. Buenos Aires: Libros en Red, 2004.

Grof, Stanislav, M.D. *The Holotropic Mind: The Three Levels of Human Consciousness and How They Shape Our Lives.* San Francisco: HarperSanFrancisco, 1990.

Guttamacher, Sally. "Whole in Body, Mind, and Spirit: Holistic Health and the Limits of Medicine." *The Hastings Center Report* 9, no. 2 (1997): 15–21.

Hall, A. Rupert. *The Revolution in Science, 1500–1750.* Boston: Addison-Wesley, 1983.

Haraway, Donna J. "A Cyborg Manifesto: Science, Technology, and Socialist-Feminism in the Late Twentieth Century." In *Simians, Cyborgs, and Women: The Reinvention of Nature,* 149–82. New York: Routledge, 1991.

Heidrich, Susan M. "Self-Discrepancy across the Life Span." *Journal of Adult Development* 6, no. 2 (1999): 119–29.

———, and Carol D. Ryff. "Physical and Mental Health in Later Life: The Self-System as Mediator," *Psychology and Aging* 8, no. 3 (1993): 327–38.

Hillman, James. *The Force of Character: And the Lasting Life.* New York: Random House, 1999.

Hubbard, Ruth. *Profitable Promises: Essays on Women, Science, and Health.* Monroe, Me.: Common Courage Press, 1995.

Hudson, Frederic M. *Adult Years: Mastering The Art of Self-Renewal.* San Francisco: Jossey-Bass, 1999.

Hudson, Joyce Rockwood. *Natural Spirituality: Recovering the Wisdom Tradition in Christianity.* Danielsville, Ga.: JRH Publications, 1998.

Hunt, Valerie. *Infinite Mind: Science of the Human Vibrations of Consciousness.* Malibu, Calif.: Malibu Publishing Company, 1996.

Iyengar, B. K. S. *Light on the Yoga Sutras of Patanjali.* London: Thorsons, 1996.

Jacobi, Jolande, *The Psychology of C. G. Jung.* 8th ed. New Haven: Yale University Press, 1973.

Johnson, Mark. *The Body in the Mind: The Bodily Basis of Meaning, Imagination, and Reason.* Chicago: University of Chicago Press, 1987.

Jones, Jill B. "Women and Their Bodies: Knowledge and Practice." Ph.D. dissertation, unpublished. Bryn Mawr, Pa.: Bryn Mawr College, 1991.

Jung, C. G. *Memories, Dreams, Reflections.* Trans. Richard and Clara Winston. New York: Vintage Books, 1963.

———. *The Structure and Dynamics of the Psyche. The Collected Works of C .G. Jung.* Vol. 8. Trans. R. F. C. Hull. Princeton: Princeton University Press, 1969.

———. *The Undiscovered Self.* Trans. R. F. C. Hull. New York: Mentor Books, 1959.

Kaye, Lenard W., and Jordan I. Kosberg, *Elderly Men: Special Problems and Professional Challenges.* New York: Springer, 1997.

Keepin, William. "Lifework of David Bohm: River of Truth." *Re-Vision,* Vol. 16, 1993. http://www.vision.net.au/~apaterson/science/david_bohm.htm.

King, P. "Notes on the psychoanalysis of older patients." *Journal of Analytical Psychology* 19 (1974): 264.

Kritchevsky, Stephen B., Ph.D., et al. "Angiotensi-Converting Enzyme Insertion/Deletion Genotype, Exercise, and Physical Decline." *Journal of the American Medical Association* 294, no. 6 (August 10, 2005): 691–98.

Kübler-Ross, Elizabeth, M.D. *The Wheel of Life: A Memoir of Living and Dying.* New York: Scribner, 1997.

Langer, Ellen. *Higher Stages of Adult Development: Perspective on Adult Growth.* New York: Oxford University Press, 1990.

Lauter, Estella, and Carol Schreier Rupprecht. *Feminist Archetypal Theory: Interdisciplinary Revisions of Jungian Thought.* Knoxville: University of Tennessee Press, 1985.

Levine, Stephen. *A Gradual Awakening.* New York: Doubleday, 1979.

Levitt, Steven D., and Stephen J. Dubner. *Freakonomics: A Rogue Economist Explores the Hidden Side of Everything.* New York: William Morrow, 2005.

Lincoln, Yvonna S., and Egon G. Guba. *Naturalistic Inquiry.* Beverly Hills, Calif.: Sage Publications, 1985.

Lipton, Bruce H. *The Biology of Belief.* Santa Rosa, Calif.: Mountain of Love/Elite Books, 2005.

Lorenzi-Prince, Ellen. *Crone Ways: In Praise of the Ancient One.* 2003. http://www.croneways.com.

Lyotard, Jean-Francois. *The Postmodern Condition: A Report on Knowledge.* Trans. Geoff Bennington and Brian Massumi. Minneapolis: University of Minnesota Press, 1993.

Maturana, Humberto R., and Francisco J. Varela. *The Tree of Knowledge: The Biological Roots of Human Understanding.* Boston: Shambhala, 1987.

McGowan, Thomas. "Ageism and Discrimination." In *Encyclopedia of Gerontology,* vol. 1, A2. Burlington, Mass.: Academic Press, 1996, 1–10.

———. "Cultural Foregrounding and the Problem of Representation: Combating Ageism through Reflexive, Intergenerational Experience." *Journal of Aging and Identity* 12, no. 4 (1997): 229–49.

McPherson, Barry. *Aging as a Social Process: An Introduction to Individual and Population Aging.* Toronto: Butterworths, 1983.

Miller, D. Patrick. "Ending My Religion." *The Sun* 313 (April 2002): 15. http://www.thesunmagazine.org/Miller316.pdf.

Ming-Dao, Deng. *365 Tao: Daily Meditations.* San Francisco: HarperSanFrancisco, 1992.

Minnich, Elizabeth Kamarck. *Transforming Knowledge.* Philadelphia: Temple University Press, 1990.

Mishler, E. C. "Meaning in Context: Is There Any Other Kind?" *Harvard Educational Review* 49, no. 1 (1979): 1–19.

Myerhoff, Barbara. *Number Our Days: Culture and Community among Elderly Jews in an American Ghetto.* New York: Simon & Schuster, 1978.

Narby, Christopher. *Against Relativism: Philosophy of Science, Deconstruction, and Critical Theory.* Malden, Mass.: Blackwell, 1997.

Nichols, Sallie. *Jung and Tarot: An Archetypal Journey.* York Beach, Me.: Samuel Weiser, 1980.

Noble, Vickie. "Artemis and Amazons." 1998. http://www.serpentina.com/origin-x.html.

Oliver, Mary. *Why I Wake Early.* Boston: Beacon Press. 2004.

Patton, Michael Quinn. *Qualitative Evaluation and Research Methods.* Newbury Park, Calif.: Sage Publications, 1990.

Pelletier, Kenneth R. *Mind as Healer, Mind as Slayer.* New York: Dell, 1977.

Prigogine, Ilya. *From Being to Becoming: Time and Complexity in the Physical Sciences.* San Francisco: W. H. Freeman and Co., 1980.

Polanyi, Michael. *Science, Faith, and Society.* Chicago: University of Chicago Press, 1964.

Polkinghorne, Donald E. *Narrative Knowing and the Human Sciences.* Albany: State University of New York Press, 1988.

Raheem, Aminah, Ph.D. *Soul Return: Integrating Body, Psyche, and Spirit.* Santa Rosa, Calif.: Aslan Publishing, 1991.

Reinharz, Shulamit. *On Becoming a Social Scientist.* San Francisco: Jossey-Bass, 1979.

Remen, Rachel Naomi, M.D. *Kitchen Table Wisdom: Stories That Heal.* New York: Riverhead, 1996.

Rosser, Sue V. "The Relationship between Women's Studies and Women in Science." In *Feminist Approaches to Science,* ed. Ruth Bleier. New York: Pergamon Press, 1986, 165–80.

Rowe, John W., and Robert L. Kahn. *Successful Aging.* New York: Pantheon Books, 1998.

Ruether, Rosemary Radford. *Religion and Sexism: Images of Women in the Jewish and Christian Traditions.* New York: Simon & Schuster, 1974.

Ryff, Carol D., Ph.D., and Victor W. Marshall, Ph.D., eds. *The Self and Society in the Aging Process.* New York: Springer, 1999.

Sadler, William A., Ph.D. *The Third Age: Six Principles for Growth and Renewal after Forty.* Cambridge, Mass.: Perseus Books, 2000.

Sarton, May. *Endgame: A Journal of the Seventy-ninth Year.* New York: W. W. Norton, 1992.

Satel, Sally, M.D. "The Indoctrinologists Are Coming." *Atlantic Monthly* 287, no. 1 (January 2001): 59–64. Adapted from her book *P.C., M.D.: How Political Correctness Is Corrupting Medicine* (New York: Basic Books, 2002).

Schlitz, Marilyn, Eugene Taylor, and Nola Lewis. "Toward a Noetic Model of Medicine." *Ions: Noetic Sciences Review* 47 (Autumn–Winter 1998). http://www.ions.org/publications/review/issue47/main.cfm?page=r47_Schlitz.html.

Schuman, Henry. *Main Currents of Scientific Thought: A History of the Sciences.* New York: S. F. Mason, 1953.

Sharma, Hari, M.D. *Awakening Nature's Healing Intelligence: Expanding Ayurveda through the Maharishi Vedic Approach to Health.* Twin Lakes, Wisc.: Lotus Press, 1997.

Shlain, Leonard. *Alphabet Versus the Goddess: The Conflict between Word and Image.* New York: Penguin/Arkana, 1999.

Siegel, Daniel J., M.D. *The Developing Mind: Toward a Neurobiology of Interpersonal Experience.* New York: Guilford Press, 1999.

Singer, Charles. *A Short History of Science to the Nineteenth Century.* London: Clarendon Press, 1941.

Snowdon, David, Ph.D. *Aging with Grace: What the Nun Study Teaches Us about Leading Longer, Healthier, and More Meaningful Lives.* New York: Bantam, 2001.

Spirduso, Waneen W. *Physical Dimensions of Aging.* Champaign, Ill: Human Kinetics, 1995.

Starr, Paul. *The Social Transformation of American Medicine.* New York: Basic Books. 1982.

Stein, Murray. *Transformation: Emergence of Self.* Carolyn and Esther Fay Series in Analytical Psychology 7. College Station: Texas A&M University Press, 1998.

Strohman, Richard C. "Genetic Determinism as a Failing Paradigm in Biology and Medicine: Implications for Health and Wellness," *Journal of Social Work Education* 39 (March 2003): 169–91.

Taimni, I. K. *The Science of Yoga: The Yoga-Sutras of Patanjali in Sanskrit.* Wheaton, Ill.: Theosophical Publishing House, 1961.

Talbot, Margaret. "The Placebo Prescription." *New York Times Magazine,* January 9, 2000.

Tart, Charles T. *Waking Up: Overcoming the Obstacles to Human Potential.* Boston: Shambhala, 1986.

Tillich, Paul. *The Courage to Be.* New Haven: Yale University Press, 1952.

Tomlinson, Richard. *From Mycenae to Constantinople: The Evolution of the Ancient City.* New York: Routledge, 1992.

Treas, Judith. "Older Americans in the 1990s and Beyond." *Population Bulletin* 50, no. 2 (May 1995). http://www.un.org/esa/population/publications/popdecline/treas.pdf. 1–11.

Turner, Barbara F., and Lillian E. Troll. *Women Growing Older: Psychological Perspectives.* Thousand Oaks, Calif.: Sage Publications, 1994.

Van Manen, Max. *Researching Lived Experience: Human Science for an Action-Sensitive Pedagogy.* Albany: State University of New York Press, 1990.

Walker, Barbara. *The Crone: Woman of Age, Wisdom, and Power.* San Francisco: HarperSanFrancisco, 1985.

Walker, Leslie G., Ph.D., and Oleg Eremin, M.D. "Psychoneuroimmunology: A New Fad or the Fifth Cancer Treatment Modality?" *The American Journal of Surgery* 170 (July 1995): 2–4.

Wilber, Ken. *The Marriage of Sense and Soul: Integrating Science and Religion.* New York: Random House, 1998.

Wolf, Fred Alan, Ph.D. *The Spiritual Universe: How Quantum Physics Proves the Existence of the Soul.* New York: Simon & Schuster, 1996.

Woodman, Marion, et al. *Leaving My Father's House: A Journey to Conscious Femininity.* Boston: Shambhala Press, 1993.

Index

depression (psychological), 7, 14, 16, 20, 74, 101, 109, 115, 123
Depression, the, 18, 32, 115, 125
Descartes, René, 19, 20, 62, 65, 70
    Cartesian/Newtonian framework, 86
Dossey, Larry, 93–94
Downing, Christine, 105
dreams, 1, 4, 17, 104, 105, 108, 113
    nightmares, 21
    of retirement, 121

Eliot, Charles William, 67
emotion, 86
    effects of, 12–13, 37, 85–87, 91, 100, 127
Erikson, Erik, 37–39, 96
etymology. *See* language

fairy tales, 110–11
faith, 47, 57, 105, 118
    in God, 5, 23, 46–47, 122, 124, 126
    in science and reason, 36–37, 62
feminist, 50
    scholars movement, 43
Foucault, Michel. *See* clinical gaze
Freud, Sigmund, 37, 40, 99–100

Galen of Perganum, 64
genetics, 35, 76, 87–88
geriatrics, 68
gerontology, 37, 65, 68, 77
gifts, 25
    from Jung, 99
    mysterious, 130
    yoga's, 127–29
Gilman, Sandra, 69
Goethe, 102
    Institute, 10
gratitude, 19, 103, 118
Grey, Aubrey D.N.J. de, 69

hag, 49, 51–52

heart
    disease, 13, 55–56, 70, 117–18
    habits of, 103
    open, 129
Heidrich, Susan, 7
Hera, 43, 56
Hippocrates, 64
holistic, 22, 58, 76, 91, 95, 96
hormones, 21
    oxytocin, 13
Hoyt, Lou, 127
hysterectomies, 70

Inquisition, 49, 52
Iyengar, B.K.S., 127–28

Jesus, 48, 55
Judaic, 43, 45, 48
Jung, Carl, 17, 47, 59, 76, 96, 98–104, 108–9

Kahn, Robert, 28, 35, 76, 121–23
Kali, 49
Kant, Immanuel, 40
Kirsh, Irving, 93
Koch, Robert, 66
Koenig, Harold, 122–23
Kornfield, Jack, 115

Langer, Ellen, 6, 35
language
    etymology, 50–51, 75
    meaning, 50
    roots of courage, 129
    word usage, 3, 5, 6, 72
Levy, Rebecca, 6
life
    expectancy, 28, 33, 95
    represented by frogs, 114
    span, 4, 40, 70
    stages, 37–40, 49, 64
    transitions, 9, 36, 39–40, 46, 66, 88, 100
Lipton, Bruce, 87
Loes, Michael, 93